RESTORE AND DRIVE

This 1953 Buick proved to be a very desirable 76-C Roadmaster convertible. Dented, with some rust in the floor pan and a gutted interior, it will require a full restoration. Available for $650, it has a potential value of $10,000–$12,000 when totally rebuilt.

RESTORE AND DRIVE

COLLECTIBLE CARS OF POSTWAR AMERICA

BOB STUBENRAUCH

PHOTOGRAPHS BY THE AUTHOR

W · W · NORTON & COMPANY

NEW YORK · LONDON

Also by Bob Stubenrauch

The Fun of Old Cars

Runabouts and Roadsters (Winner of the Thomas McKean Memorial Cup 1973)

Where Freedom Grew

Published simultaneously in Canada by
Penguin Books Canada Ltd,
2801 John Street, Markham, Ontario L3R 1B4.

The text of this book is composed in Trump Mediaeval, with display type set in Avant Garde Gothic X-light.
Composition by The Vail-Ballou Press, Inc. Manufacturing by The Murray Printing Company.
Book design by Jacques Chazaud

Library of Congress Cataloging in Publication Data

Stubenrauch, Bob.
Restore and drive

Bibliography: p. 191
1. Automobiles—Conservation and restoration.
I. Title.
TL152.2.S78   1984   629.28'722   83–25462

ISBN 0-393-01874-1

W. W. Norton & Company, Inc., 500 Fifth Avenue, New York, N.Y. 10110
W. W. Norton & Company Ltd., 37 Great Russell Street, London WC1B 3NU

2 3 4 5 6 7 8 9 0

For my sons,
David and Bruce,
and my grandson,
Ryan Matthew Stubenrauch

CONTENTS

ACKNOWLEDGMENTS

I wish to thank the following for their generous cooperation:

Keith Poyser, owner of the 1946 Ford; Greg Olekszak, owner of the 1947 Packard; Robert Dierkesheide, owner of the 1948 Town and Country; David and Dell Moell, owners of the 1948 Olds; Garlton Adams, owner of the 1949 Studebaker; Bob Porter, owner of the 1951 Chrysler and the 1953 Imperial limo; Jack Schoonover, owner of the 1951 Cadillac; Dwayne Stone, owner of the 1951 Hudson; Dr. Herbert Mahler, owner of the 1953 Olds; Ken Liska, owner of the 1953 Buick; Cal and Lori Middleton, owners of the 1954 DeSoto; John James, owner of the 1954 Mercury; Joyce Talcott, owner of the 1955 Nomad wagon; "Woody" Majors, owner of the 1956 Packard; Ken Vanderbush, owner of the 1960 Rambler; John Glassner, owner of the 1961 Lincoln; Tom McGuinness, owner of the 1963 Pontiac; Marilyn Daniels, owner of the 1963 Imperial; Craig Badger, owner of the 1963 Thunderbird; Tom Schweitzer, owner of the 1964 Plymouth; Dennis Bowsher, owner of the 1966 Mustang; and Stuart Middleton, owner of the 1967 Plymouth GTX.

For their work in preparing their cars for the photo sessions, in some cases removing them from storage, and for their patience, I am most grateful.

FOREWORD

Since the mid-sixties the old-car hobby has changed as dramatically as have the new cars themselves. In 1965 I started to write my first book on the subject, published in 1967 as *The Fun of Old Cars*. Intending to give a comprehensive overview of the field, I note now that I treated only one postwar auto, under the special interest category. Virtually half the work was devoted to antique cars, the other half to classics. At that time the four-door Lincoln convertibles were still in production, and the two-seater Thunderbirds only eight years out of production. With the muscle car market booming, the only foreign inroads into the Detroit fiefdom were British sports cars and a scattering of luxury autos such as Mercedes and Rolls.

It has been over forty years since the period during which all auto production ceased in America as Detroit, South Bend, and Kenosha went to war in those grim days after Pearl Harbor. When victory came, there was a pent-up demand for new cars—and wartime earnings to buy them. Many consider the immediate postwar period thru the sixties a golden age for Detroit's products. Certainly the cars of no two makers looked alike. Each had a distinctive personality, and any teenage boy who couldn't tell a 1950 Nash from a 1950 Ford four blocks away might well hang his head in shame.

Volume car production in America dates as far back as 1910, making the post–World War II era only about five years longer than our entire prior auto history. It has been a richly productive period, however, and the postwar flood of diversity in automobile design—the fruit of over two dozen different makers—has created a growing legion of admirers. A more recent development in the industry is the collection of all domestic auto production under just five name plates, two of which (Volkswagen of America and AMC-Renault) exist on foreign capital.

In the fifties you could shop showrooms of makers that are now just hazy memories: Hudson and Nash, Kaiser and Studebaker, Willys, Crosley, DeSoto and Packard. What car will you seek for restoring? One of these "orphan" makes, or a product of one of the original companys' survivor offshoots? You may be driven by nostalgia. Perhaps the Buick Roadmaster that Dad drove you to Lake Placid in, or maybe the Rocket 88 Olds you took years later on your honeymoon. Or drawn by admiration for impressive engineering and "Star Wars" styling, you may select a '59 Cadillac convertible. Like an increasing number of hobbyists today who prefer appreciation to depreciation, your restored collectible might become the family's main car. For that kind of room and comfort you would consider a '54 Chrysler New Yorker or a '64 Pontiac Bonneville. Once, only a retired mechanic would have been able to answer the "missing-part" question—and an overgrown wrecking yard hold that vital part—but today's collector can find a whole army of support systems.

First, there are the clubs, scores of them, most with regional chapters in every state. Many are built around one make, some even around one brief period of one make. Then there are the major hobby periodicals, such as *Hemmings Motor News, Old Cars Weekly,* and *Cars and Parts.* The most significant aid the restorer of a postwar car has today, virtually unknown in the thirties, is the huge reproduction parts industry. It is no exaggeration to say that a '65 Mustang or a '57 Chevrolet could be built from the frame up with newly made reproduction parts: from floor pan to dashpad to correct-to-the-last-thread upholstery.

Whatever you hope to find, acquire a general knowledge of all makes. You may pass up the chance of a lifetime because you had your sights set too rigidly on that one certain model. And further, you will constantly be surprised at the bright ideas car makers came up with in this most competitive era. Not all these autos are imposing and impressive, but surely they are all interesting—and they represent an age that can never return. No cars for the masses will ever be this large and heavy, this varied in style, this lavish of chrome, this shamelessly opulent in comfort, this powerful in performance. The oil embargo of 1973 rang down the curtain on this auto age. Cars today, the econobox we need for the now-precious fluid we call gasoline, are half the weight and triple the cost. It is barely conceivable that future generations will collect these vehicles, but we have a better choice; they are hiding in barns and sleeping under dust covers, each with its own history, its own story. An American family once built lives and vacations (and budgets!) around one of these cars waiting to be discovered, restored, and taken back to the highway. The cars we built here in those busy years after victory are a legacy. Thousands of new hobbyists are finding a thrill in preserving that legacy, and deep satisfaction in that moment when they turn the ignition key and a long dead auto comes to life again.

CHAPTER ONE

"Right" Cars and "Wrong" Cars

Not all old cars are collectible. Some problem-plagued old cars are more desirable than many well-engineered, fine-running old models. Some that were very expensive when new cost even more today, while others that were once costly can be had, sound and running, for 10 percent of their original list price.

How each old-car model is priced has much to do with its present popularity. Hence the 1965–66 Mustang commands high prices despite an enormous number available, because many, many people want one. Compare a solid 1965 Mustang, one of nearly half a million made, to a 1958 Packard hardtop coupe (not Hawk) in similarly solid condition. The Packard model is historic because 1958 was the last year for the make; it is an attractive hardtop produced in just 675 copies. Yet the current price range is $1,000–3,000 for the Packard versus $3,000–5,000 for the Mustang.

Scarcity is a factor in pricing, but a low-production car that never became popular when new will probably never excite a great demand among hobbyists. The exceptions are specialty cars, such as the Nash-Healey roadster and the Muntz and Kurtis sports cars.

The general rules governing popularity of the classic cars of the thirties apply also to postwar cars. Convertibles are most in demand, followed by two-door hardtops, then come unusual body styles, such as torpedo or fastback coupes, followed by all other two-door models. Four-door hardtops are ahead of four-door sedans, and long-wheelbase limos bring up the rear. One no sooner says this than exceptions come to mind. Why is the Nomad wagon of Chevrolet one of the hottest collectibles around? It is hard to understand when other attractive wagons go begging, such as the Rambler Cross Country models and the majestic yacht-sized Chrysler Town and Country wagons of 1953–54.

A rare 1952 DeSoto V-8 convertible. That is a factory continental kit, and those are genuine wire wheels. Damp storage over a twenty-year period caused extensive rust, and a total frame-up restoration on this rare model is needed.

In addition to body style, another key criterion for determining a model's collectibility is styling innovation, regardless of mechanical perfection. Examples might include the 1953 Studebaker sport coupes and hardtops; the first true hardtops in 1949 of Oldsmobile, Cadillac, and Buick; along with other makes that came later, such as the 1952 Lincoln. It does not follow that these styling innovations were, and are, universally admired. Who today would claim the 1949 Nash Airflyte a thing of beauty? The "bathtub" Nash, as it was quickly dubbed, was a strong leap forward in auto design, being far more aerodynamically shaped than the competition. Like the homely Chrysler Airflow of 1934, however, it has belatedly earned its place in the logbook of genuine engineering advances.

If the bathtub Nash was a styling leader in 1949, it became so with a very conventional engine and frame. Sometimes engineering innovations go hand in glove with bold, new design styling, and sometimes dramatic breakthroughs are practically invisible. The front-wheel drive Toronado of 1966 introduced a new approach to the whole drive and suspension of a car with a striking new body design. The same applies to the Cadillac Eldorado of 1967 and its version of front-wheel drive innovation.

By contrast, Cadillac electrified the industry and drew showroom crowds with its new overhead valve V-8 engine in the 1949 line. Strangely enough, the car's body was so like that of the 1948 model it was hard to tell them apart. Chrysler soon made a name for itself with the "hemi" engine, introduced in 1951, but put it in stodgy, boxy sedans for four long years. They finally got the message that fine engineering deserves up-to-date styling.

The last rule of thumb for collectors is that low-production, top-of-the-line cars are usually worth seeking out. The Mark II Lincoln Continental of 1956–57 is a good example. The standard long wheelbase Fleetwood Caddys of the sixties are a bad example. Costing nearly as much when new as the MK II, these 75 series models are too big for most hobbyists and are now available at a fifth of the price of the Lincoln. But if one checks the top models of, for example, Packard, the expensive Caribbeans from 1953 to 1956 are the most sought after postwar cars they made. Studebaker's Avanti was a bargain when new (though a high-priced, top-of-the-line model for that maker) and is now breaking the $10,000 mark.

The careful collector of old cars must both accept the fact that there are rules and criteria for every car and be prepared to ignore those guideposts when other factors prevail. Does one reject a desirable 1953 Buick Skylark because it is priced over the market, or does its having gone into storage when just thirty months old change one's mind?

Fortunately, there are available cars that meet all the benchmarks for solid investments at reasonable prices. Protection of your dollar investment is not the prime reason for being in any hobby, but it certainly makes more sense to restore a desirable car rather than an oddball of very limited appeal. Interest in vintage cars solely as investment portfolio additions has clouded the plain fun of earlier days. It has also led to waves of interest in certain cars, causing them to be "hot" one year and "cold" the next. The four-door Lincoln converts of 1961–67 are a case in point. In the late seventies mint condition models were approaching $10,000. Now they

Attending the larger old-car meets will introduce the newcomer to the whole span of motoring including cars such as this brass-age Lozier.

Barn stored since 1956, this 1953 Buick Skylark is a low-production, low-mileage find. It would be considered a very easy restoration project.

seem to have returned to the $4,000-to-$6,500 range. With this high-pressure money activity, it makes sense to do your homework carefully before buying a restored car at auction. There are many reputable firms in this field, but the level of sophistication in "replicating" scarce models is astonishing. Because a 1960 Edsel convertible is rare (76 units represent total production), look-a-like Ford convertibles have been artfully converted into fake Edsels. A few pieces of trim and a fiberglass tonneau can change a plain-Jane T'bird convert into the very scarce and more valuable Sports Roadster of 1962–63. Will each one of these conversions be honestly described as it is resold over the years? As always, the buyer should know what he is getting. Researching serial numbers can save many wasted dollars.

All of the above notwithstanding, each person's choice will come more from the heart than the brain, as the determining factors become very subjective to a neophyte peering into his first dusty garage, shifting the furniture aside, and turning down the old quilt on the long-covered hood. He may have started out looking for a Chevy Nomad or a Plymouth Fury, but when the big chrome wings appear, and then the huge length of that 1953 Chrysler Imperial Newport hardtop coupe comes into view, strange things happen. A Mopar buff may have been created in five minutes of excitement.

Because so much of this hobby depends simply on personal preference, I feel obliged to pass along my favorites—some I have owned, others I still seek. At the conclusion of each car profile, I'll indicate models of that make that have aroused my interest over the years. Some are popular, some would be classified as "sleepers," and some may never develop a following. Look over the gleaming rows at your next old-car show, and decide for yourself.

16

CHAPTER TWO
Old Cars Found in Barns
(Some should be left there!)

t is easy to say: first learn how to shop, do your homework—then worry about exactly where to shop for the old car you're seeking. Unfortunately, the car buff who has totally succumbed to the mania of the hobby is always shopping. That is, he may not be able to find the salad dressing section in the supermarket but he can spot the tail fins of a '59 Cadillac in an overgrown back yard a mile from the highway. Like a skilled bird watcher, the committed car hobbyist has developed his peripheral vision and sharpened his hearing: both senses attuned to things old and automotive.

It is surprising how many owners at a car meet will confide that they found their automotive gem when they weren't even looking. Usually this happens because for years they have regaled their non-hobbyist friends with tales of their automotive interest, and those friends provide tips about old cars becoming available. That is the simplest first step in your hunt, let your friends know.

In brief, you have a number of possible routes, from both within the hobby and outside it. At one time more bargains probably were found outside the hobby. But now that the general public has become more aware of the restoration mania, the assumption is that all cars old enough to vote are worth many thousands of dollars. I recently inspected a 1958 Edsel hauled out of a decade of neglected storage. Restoration was still possible, but at very high cost due to massive rust out of the door pillars and wheel wells. It was difficult for the owner to accept my belief that his car was suitable only for parts.

If you already know just what you want, look first in the hobby. That will involve subscribing to two or three of the leading periodicals listed in the back of this book. It might come as a surprise that in one issue of *Hemmings Motor News* you may find twenty pages of Ford ads alone. Investigate the clubs, join the nearest regional chapter, and comb both the national and local bulletins for the car you seek. Joining a club that

This Packard has a decent body shell, but the rockers and floor are heavily rotted. Restoration would be possible but at a higher cost than this particular model might justify.

includes hundreds of other hobbyists who are also dedicated to your specific car is the best route to finding everything from parts to restoration advice about that model.

Faithfully attending every car meet you can get to will give you the broad general knowledge you need to fully enjoy the hobby of old-car restoration. Seeing well-restored examples of various makes will help you determine your own preferences. Some hobbyists collect sales literature and magazine ads for both pleasure and education.

The other prime source of cars within the hobby is at auction. This can be a local affair,

run perhaps by a reputable civic group or by a regional museum. Normal caution and standard business common sense should suffice here. It is at the national (or international) auction events, where five hundred cars may be run past the block over several days, that more care is necessary. Not to say that you will be flim-flammed, but these events attract "fake" cars, as well as "fake" buyers who sometimes can't pay for their purchases, and sellers who know all the tricks to bring the bidding to unrealistically high levels. Some years ago I attended an auction run by a highly reputable house that was new to the handling of classic cars. They sold a Rolls Royce and decently took it back an hour later when experts present pointed out it had been represented as original when in fact it sported a poorly made, nonauthentic replica body. In this case, both the buyer and auctioneer had been misled. Make sure of what you want to spend, make sure of the car's condition, and make sure you get a valid title—and buying a car at auction can be a happy experience.

I have purchased cars from hobbyists who advertised in the leading periodicals but admit to finding more pleasure in doing my own detective work and finding the "undiscovered" car. This approach involves many unsuccessful trips for each one that turns up a worthwhile car. Occasionally that rare car is one I can't afford or have no special interest in. I then suggest how the owner should advertise it and feel some satisfaction in bringing another lost car back into the mainstream of the hobby.

Where should you look outside the hobby to turn up that hidden-away old car? You might start with the obvious place, the used-car lots. Most dealers don't want collectibles, but they sometimes accept them as trade-ins. After a month of trying to get the highest figure in *Old Cars Weekly Price Guide,* they may listen to a realistic offer. Over one weekend recently, I checked out a dozen local lots to test this theory and found the following: a '58 Olds sedan, a

A 1960 Thunderbird goes on the auction block at a regional old-car meet in Ohio.

A first-year 1966 Olds Toronado goes on the block at a nationally advertised auction. Bidders rarely get to talk to car owners, much less drive the car at these high-pressure events.

This 1952 Cadillac convertible was offered at $500 seven years ago. It would probably command $3,000 today.

Old cars surface anywhere. This senior series Mercedes appeared at roadside for sale as is.

'64 Lincoln Continental, a '62 Buick Special, a '56 Lincoln Premiere, and a '62 Lincoln four-door convertible. Prices were within reason, though none the amazing buy I found in 1976, when I spotted a 1966 four-door Lincoln convertible: wearing a tattered top and parked in the "transportation special" row of a small dealer, it was priced at exactly $197.

You might also alert a local new-car dealer to call you if he gets an old-car trade-in. Some dealers would prefer a quick sale without the trouble of "prepping" an old car. A Chevy dealer

This clean-looking 1964 Buick Riviera was a bargain at $300. Unfortunately it sat idle on a dirt driveway for three years and had extensive rustout in the floor pan and trunk area.

will naturally get more Camaros in trade, an old-line Chrysler dealer will be more likely to get an old Imperial, and so forth.

House-and-contents auctions are another fine source of old cars. No less than a dozen old cars were found recently in two pages of this type of ad, buried in the fine print, in my hometown Sunday paper. Many times such auctions are "absolute," with no reserve, and few car buffs will be in attendance. A decent step-down Hudson brought just fifty dollars at one of these auctions a few years ago.

Comb the classified ads under Household Goods and Miscellaneous. I went to inspect a 1965 Cutlass at a moving sale last year and found the owner had not thought it important on a two-hundred-dollar car sale to mention that the car was a convertible!

You can, of course, place your own classified ad, giving the years and makes you arc seeking. This usually draws replies from other hobbyists but is worth trying in your area. If you don't want to be awakened at midnight with the exciting details of Aunt Molly's rust-free Gremlin, rent a post office box for replies.

One last guideline: it seems the more cars a person has to sell, the cheaper any one of them will be. Check out this theory by looking over the "mixed make" columns in *Hemmings* or the multiple cars list in *Old Cars Weekly*. The Hudson one individual prices at $1200 may go for $400 if it is one of sixty unrestored cars offered because the farm is being sold for a housing development. A recent auction in Nebraska saw cars well worth at least $1,000 go for from $100 to $400 each.

The really dedicated (or perhaps "foolhardy" is the word) hobbyist is the fellow who will tow a trailer two or three hundred miles to an auction, on the slight chance he may buy a car. One

A long-closed wrecking yard turned up this original 1953 Studebaker Loewy hardtop, with many usable parts intact.

A streamlined Buick sedanet in a small wrecking yard for sale complete, as the owner believed it to be quite restorable.

This pair of Nash Metropolitans is a wrecking-yard find. Both appear eminently restorable.

collector says he takes his trailer "everywhere" just so he will be ready when he spots that abandoned Avanti out in the meadow.

Let's assume you have found a car that interests you. The price seems right, and you are ready to close the deal. Have you really inspected that car? Have you run down a list and made a ball-park estimate of exactly what is needed? Or have you bought an old convertible phaeton and waited until you got it home to inspect the glass? Turning the crank and finding there are no windows to run up can be discouraging. One buyer didn't notice the engine fan was missing, once home he finally noticed the crankshaft was

missing as well. The problem of missing parts can be serious right up to models from the early seventies. In general, engine and mechanical parts are easier to obtain than missing trim pieces from low-production models. On high-production, high-priced cars, such as Corvettes, they are available—but the prices may drive you back to stamp collecting.

One reason Ford and Chevrolet models are popular as "first project" cars is the relative ease of obtaining parts for them. Before you go to hobby sources, try the older auto supply houses in your area. My order of search is usually: local houses, hobby periodical ads, club bulletin ads, western wrecking yards. I will keep notes on decent, intact older cars I spot in local wrecking yards. Solid bumper ends for fifties Cadillacs are much sought after because the tail pipe exiting through the bumper caused early rustout. A pair through a hobby supplier currently is over $200. The local yard asks $35 for the entire bumper. I found a pair of mint Thunderbird fender skirts in a local yard: hobby cost is about $50 per pair, these were just $6.

If money is no object, you will probably never set foot in a wrecking yard, and you may miss some rare sights, such as a yard with fourteen Lincoln Zephyrs in one corner.

Choosing between a decent interior with a sound body, accompanied by mechanical problems, and a smooth-running car that has heavy rustout, I would always prefer the sound car with mechanical problems.

It is very expensive to duplicate the factory interior of a fifties car, and many times the final "look" will not be right, even though the material and patterns are correct. Find an original mint Packard, Cadillac, or Olds of the late forties or early fifties, look at the workmanship, and you will understand why duplicating it may cost in excess of two or three thousand dollars.

If you become familiar with the model you are shopping for, you have the advantage of knowing its weaknesses. If it is a Studebaker

A rare 1947 Cadillac convertible leaves the barn for a new home and restoration.

This pair of Studebaker Lark convertibles was offered by a hobbyist with too many projects on hand. One could be restored easily from the two.

This 1950 Plymouth looks deceptively sound. Severely rotted underneath, it was a very good parts car.

hardtop or Hawk of the fifties, you will start at the fender and door post. Faulty design trapped moisture here, and it is a rare car that does not have rot in this area. Take up the rugs and rear seats. Sometimes the carpet is almost the only thing left between you and a view of the gound. Don't let a car's good points sway your judgment when you know major problems exist as well. Try to be objective and total up the worst possible scenario of costs.

Some years ago I purchased a 1950 Plymouth convertible, a delightful compact-sized beauty with a neat dash and nice original upholstery. The owner kept describing it as a "parts car." The fenders, grille, and bumpers were fine, the inside really nice. I tried to ignore the spongy feel underfoot as I stepped into the car. I over-looked the need to lift the doors to close them. I disregarded the large rust holes in the trunk and bought it—a genuine parts car!

Close inspection revealed the honest owner was right. Neither door post had a bottom, the whole car sagged with the open doors not holding it up, and almost none of the floor was solid. It required a knowledgeable, frame-up restoration. I was fortunate in finding two men who had just completed restoring the same model and wanted to tackle another. I gratefully sold it to them.

You may learn more from a close inspection of a derelict of the model you like than from a restored example. Mustangs are a case in point. The catalog of repro parts being made today may convince you the only part that doesn't rust out on the early Mustang is the windshield. Inspect hulks in wrecking yards and you will find certain areas go first. If those places are sound on the car you're considering, you can reasonably assume other hidden areas are still sound.

One last comment on hard-to-find parts: It is human nature to charge what the market will bear. Certain rare accessories, grilles, and trim may be available at what seem like prohibitive prices. But these pricetags are not necessarily the norm. I have seen the prized Thunderbird wire wheels for the Sports Roadster of 1962 go for $400 each in fine condition. Recently a set of these N.O.S. wheels were advertised at $4,000. Even a 99-point show car might not justify that difference. Before you buy the rare goody your car needs, shop enough to know the fair mid-range, because the asking range will vary enormously. I recently got three quotes on a 1942 Cadillac grille, a scarce item, as Caddy production in that war year was very low. One quote was for a decent grille with usable chrome at $95. The second quote was for a rusty but straight and replateable grille at $125. The third was for a cracked, broken, *and* rusty grille at $300. All prices were firm. I am now convinced of the need to shop around for the best value.

A solid 1964 Lincoln that has lost its motor, wheels, and hood, it still has many parts to contribute in this auto graveyard.

On the question of pricing an unrestored old car, today's hobbyist has the advantage of several price guides and frequently published auction results. Some prices in *Old Cars Price Guide* seem low to me, others unduly high. Across the board, they indicate useful ballpark figures but become really valuable when the seller is accurate about the car's condition. In the end, it still comes down to what a seller will accept, and how high the prospective buyer is willing to go. If you want a complete and sound '65 Mustang convertible, you are in the seller's market, as he has a hot and desirable car. If you find a 1949 eight-passenger, long-wheelbase Chrysler Windsor limousine, on the other hand, the seller

may throw in his daughter's hand in marriage, as he has a car of low demand. He will show you the car in a ballpark to make it look smaller and lie thru his teeth that it *will* fit in your garage. Some people, however, would be prouder to have one of seventy-three made, rather than, as the Mustang owner, share his model with over half a million others.

Some cars found in barns should be left right there, others are well worth months, or years, of effort to rescue and restore them. Until you roll that weathered door back and examine the car revealed, you won't know if this will be the one for you. This is why the real car lover follows every lead and explores every find. You won't buy every car you see, but the stories you hear are themselves usually worth the trip!

CHAPTER THREE

The Three Roads to Restoration

At this point you have located and purchased the car you intend to restore. You will be taking one of the following three routes to restoration:

1. A full-service restoration shop will do the entire job. You have checked their references and closely examined several cars under restoration in their shop. You will have visited at least one of their customers and discussed his experience with the shop. They have told you in writing how they charge: that is, the rate for mechanical work, for parts-hunting, and so forth. They have given you an estimate with certain guarantees. You are not committed to a total restoration with an open-end figure. If the shop has advertised for some time in a publication like *Hemmings Motor News,* you have asked the magazine if they have had complaints or praise of the shop's work. Finally, you have compared the cost of their restoration with the value of the finished car.

2. You are going to tackle the job yourself. You have the mechanical skills and a place to work. (Minimum is usually a two-car garage.) You may employ a machine shop and a paint shop and have the interior professionally reupholstered, but all other work you will perform yourself.

This is the ultimate achievement, and thousands of individuals have done it. Stock brokers and doctors, teachers and mailmen, as well as auto mechanics, many have restored cars from the frame up.

3. Probably the most common and, for the majority, most logical approach: in effect, you become the sub-contractor of this multi-skill project. You may do a portion of the disassembly, such as removing all trim and glass. You

This 1956 Golden Hawk yielded several trim parts for the author's Power Hawk project. Wrecking-yard finds are usually lower priced than those in the old-car hobby outlets.

may take easily removable sheet metal off—hood, deck lid, and doors—and take them to the sand blaster or dip tank.

You may remove all the interior, take everything to the upholstery shop. They may ask you to obtain the materials if it can only be matched through hobby sources. Every part you can find reduces your bill for the service fee you would otherwise be paying to someone else.

At some point, you will need the services of a good body shop for the reassembly of components. Try to find a place that respects what you are doing. The large-volume shop doing collision work on late models only is probably not that place. A shop that works at a measured pace will understand your goal better. Perhaps someone in your local old-car club has a recommendation. The same applies to selecting the

Bringing a grimy 1965 convertible T'bird out of the barn. Collectors learn to look past the dust and chicken droppings!

Stripping out the sodden carpets in this Riviera trunk revealed serious rust problems. Obviously, it pays to do this before confirming your purchase of the car you're considering.

This nearly rust-free 1948 Cadillac convertible was offered at $1,750 in 1978. Restored value then was around $5,000, about a third of today's market value.

commercial shops for brake work, convertible tops, and chrome plating.

It may not be possible, but is certainly desirable, to begin work only when you have obtained all the missing parts you're aware of. Some hobbyists with several old cars awaiting restoration shop the flea markets with a list of what is needed. Each part goes in the trunk of the car as it is found and checked off a list taped to the windshield. When all the problem items are crossed off, restoration can begin.

Finding parts, particularly for postwar cars, is easier today than it was a decade ago. The rapid growth of the one-make car clubs and the increasing number of people who deal in parts as a full-time business have helped enormously. Most parts can be found through ads in the leading hobby periodicals. Ads in the club publications are valuable because they will relate exclusively to your make auto. Other sources are the western and southern wrecking yards. Out of the rust belt, sheet metal seems to last forever, and far from the steel mills, the scrap car crusher is seldom employed. Many of the larger yards with older cars advertise in *Hemmings Motor News*.

Whether you do the whole restoration or part of it yourself, or send it out, or buy it as a completed restoration, the more you see of the work in progress, the better you will understand your car's qualities and its quirks on the highway.

CHAPTER FOUR
You Can Drive These Investments

Most owners of collectible cars in pristine condition do not drive them every day but keep them for summertime, weekend vehicles. We have all, however, become energy conscious and note each rise in the price of gas with a twinge. As a nation of drivers, we are reconciled to our econobox transportation, or are we?

There seems to be a small but growing movement, a few families here and there in every neighborhood, who are back in the fifties to stay. Mom and Dad have sold the econobox, or given it to Daughter for school commuting, and go everywhere in the '57 Chevy Bel Air. A local business-district parking-lot attendant will see these cars pull in every day: a '55 Buick Super, a '61 Lincoln, a '67 Eldorado, a '65 Mustang, a '55 Chevy, a '51 Caddy convertible. All are gleaming, restored cars, and all obviously are giving the owners satisfaction in everyday use.

I anticipate this movement will grow as more old-car owners realize that the rate of depreciation on a new car far exceeds the higher operating costs of a typical collectible of the postwar era. Some of us just never could reconcile the loss of comfort and room, view, and feel of security, for the gas-saving benefit of a small, noisy, and cramped vehicle.

If you are debating whether to make a restored collectible your family's "first" car, consider the following:

Will I have a parts problem?

Can it be worked on by a mechanic not familiar with it?

Is it likely to go up in value?

Is it practical for my needs?

Can it perform on today's gasoline?

The answer to the first question should be no, if you do some planning. You can do what owners of the thirties' classics do when they travel across the country to a national show—take along spares. You should consider having in your trunk the following parts, ready for an emergency: fuel pump, water pump, upper and lower radiator hoses, heater hose, fan and generator belts, and owner's and shop manuals. If you have

an unusual braking system, such as Chrysler's early disc devices, you might want parts or a rebuild kit for that. You should know where your fuses are and have a set of spares. Other than these precautions, you should be no more at risk of a breakdown than any other motorist.

In answer to the second question, the average mechanic would sooner work on a '55 Chevy than an '82 Chevy. In the pre-electronic age of these collectible cars, everything is basically the same and far more accessible. If it is a complicated problem, having the shop manual at hand will certainly help.

Will my fifties' car go up in value? It seems that when the country is in recession, old-car values may stagnate, but they don't collapse. When the economy is thriving, collectible cars have been seen to outstrip the inflation rate in appreciation. Like any collectible, some old cars are more in demand and rise faster in value than others. Right now, any 1965–67 Mustang, any 1955–57 Chevy, any Pontiac GTO 1964–66—carefully restored and driven—simply will not *lose* value. It *may* increase in value from 10 percent to 15 percent per year as more people and more investors joing the hobby.

It is fascinating to guess which cars will move from sleeper to red hot. My own list of underpriced and underappreciated cars would include the following candidates for future appreciation:

- Crown Imperial convertibles 1957–1968
  Only four hundred to six hundred of these huge, great-handling convertibles were made each year. At the present range of $1,000 to

More and more cars of the sixties are appearing at car meets. This is the very collectible 1964 Buick Riviera.

An exceptionally solid 1961 Lincoln that had been rustproofed when new. Repair of dents in the door and a new exhaust system were its principal requirements.

This 1948 Chevrolet coupe appeared for sale out of decades of dead storage. It would be classified as an "easy" restoration project.

$3,000 for unrestored examples, they should have a bright future.

- Cadillac Eldorado coupe 1967–1970
  More interest is displayed in the Olds Toronado of the same period and similar front-wheel–drive engineering than in this magnificent Cadillac. Fewer than 18,000 were made in '67 and the first-year model will be most sought after although the '70 Eldo is the most powerful Caddy ever made: 400 HP at 500-cubic-inch displacement! Current prices I've seen range from $150 to $800 for restorable cars, and a 1967 model cream puff gem at $1,800.

- Cadillac Eldorado Seville hardtop coupe 1956–1960
  It is a mystery to me that the Eldo Biarritz convertibles have gone off the charts (over $10,000) and the companion hardtops languish in the cellar. I've seen several '57 and '58 Sevilles under $1,000 recently, and $2,000 buys a decent driver. Production averaged 900 units each year, and with only 50 to 75 survivors per model, these rare and opulent cars should catch on shortly.

At a local annual old-car auction, this solid and clean 1956 Chrysler St. Regis hardtop was obtainable in the $3,000 range.

- Buick Riviera sport coupe 1966–1969

  This second series still takes a back seat with collectors to the near-classic 1963–1965 beauty. Many can be found as third-owner transportation cars in the $300-to-$1,000 price range. A mint 1967 Riviera drew the crowds away from the 'Vettes and Mustangs at a recent show. Produced in large numbers, parts are no problem. It should come along over the next few years.

- Chrysler Imperial hardtop coupes 1953–1956

  These four years bridged a dramatic change in body style. The '53 and '54 are classic boxy Chrysler styles of 1950 origin, elegant on the long wheelbase of 131.5 inches. Powered by the big hemi engine and superbly trimmed, they are available in the $600-to-$1,500 range in unrestored condition.

The '55 and '56 have the "new" look, rounded and streamlined with possibly the cleanest and most aristocratic grille on a postwar American car. These great road cars run only slightly higher, with restored examples at around $4,000. Yearly production ranged from 800 to 2,000, which means nice trim parts are scarce.

While the above models may move up sharply in value in the future, certain cars are today great value for the money—although it seems unlikely they will ever soar. Where initial outlay is a concern, all of the following have been seen recently in the price range *under* $1,000 in fair to very good unrestored shape.

Imperial sedans, Crown & LeBaron: 1957–1968
Studebaker sedans: 1953–1964
Rambler sedans and wagons:1956–1962
Lincoln sedans: 1952–1956
Buick sedans: 1954–1957
Buick Skylark wagon: 1965
Imperial sedans and coupes: 1969–1973
Buick Riviera "boattail": 1971–1973

These are all interesting cars, and some represent incredible buys. The early Buicks and Ramblers are very easy on gas, while the latter-day Rivieras and LeBaron Imperials are in the 12-MPG area. Ironically, a Studebaker four-door sedan at a car show is a curiosity. So many hobbyists restore the hardtops and Hawks that a restored sedan is becoming rare.

Our remaining concerns on driving a collectible every day—is it practical, and is today's gasoline suitable—are easily answered.

Obviously, a Corvette is not ideal for the large family with only one car. Other than size, everything we take for granted in today's cars was in 80 percent of the fifties' cars. Power steering arrived in 1952, and most makes offered it by 1955. Power brakes, electric windows, and, of course, air conditioning were around soon after the postwar car boom developed. It takes a little time to adjust to the larger steering wheels in use then. Vision over the road was probably better due to the higher seat position. You may want to replace slow or erratic vacuum windshield wipers with electric units, but that is easily done. You may want a tape player, but mini units are made that will mount out of sight in that roomy glove box.

With only 28,000 miles on its odometer, this 1958 Chrysler New Yorker hardtop was offered recently for $325. A sound running car, it carries the last-offered version of the legendary hemi engine.

A rare sight anywhere: the Road Runner Superbird was the ultimate in fins and muscle, and few of the 2,000 made in 1970 are still around.

If you are driving a big-engine, high-compression muscle car, you may have a fuel problem. It is no secret that the gasoline available today has lower octane. One solution was recently discussed at length in several of the car buff magazines. When the tank is filled with an equal mixture of leaded gasoline (regular at about 89 octane) and premium lead-free gas (at about 93 or 94 octane) a synergistic chemical reaction occurs that actually raises the octane of the blend to a few numbers over the highest octane put in, something like 96 or 97 octane. This approaches the level of high test, or premium gasoline used in the fifties and sixties. The engine should be tuned on this mixture, and while gassing up will be a minor nuisance, the car should run reasonably well and still receive enough lead to protect the valves. One routine a friend follows is fueling at the appropriate alternate pumps every time the gas gauge drops to half full. This technique keeps the blend roughly equal in the tank.

Obviously, millions of Americans are not about to turn the clock back and the highways into a rerun of "Happy Days," but it is nice to know that your collectible is a usable artifact—for whatever distance you may care to drive it—which is just what the maker had in mind in the first place.

CHAPTER FIVE
Limos Go in Style

European bigwigs never had difficulty adjusting to block-long limousines, I'm sure. After all, for people accustomed to royal carriages and footmen, it was a logical development. Once the motorcar had become a familiar sight in America, however, the limo was a problem for some of our wealthy. It seemed such an ostentatious way to flaunt wealth and position. In the depression, when millions worried more about soles on their shoes than tires on their cars, limos were out. Brewster sold a few hundred humble Fords with fancy grilles so his lordship, the banker, could go to his Fifth Avenue club in disguise, as it were. Buick had great success with a run of limo models in the late thirties. They were longer than stock sedans but retiring in their decor, and as one owner put it: "Yes, it's a limousine, but only a Buick."

In the postwar period, along with prosperity, flaunting it was back in—and quite American. Cadillac picked up production of its formal 75

series; Packard made limos available; and Chrysler worked on the lower end of the market. DeSoto and Dodge offered eight-passenger sedans, and Imperial was a prestige name for the long wheelbase models. There was even a market that had nothing to do with snobbery: An eight-passenger car was a necessity for resorts— ideal for meeting the train and transporting guests. The corporate customer was now far more common than the private buyer who kept a full-time liveried chauffeur.

Early in the fifties another interesting change occurred. This was the limo treatment given to a stock luxury sedan. While Chrysler made a full-sized eight-passenger limo on a 139-inch wheelbase in 1953, they also offered an Imperial Town Limousine, which was a reworked version of the standard Imperial sedan, on the regular wheelbase. This dandy car was finished in leather up front and in fine broadcloth in the rear. The rear compartment had its own heater, reading lamps, and of course an electric divider

An interesting story went with this 1952 Series 75 Cadillac limo: The owner believed its first owner was Mrs. Harry Truman but lacked documentary proof. The car was quite sound and restorable.

window. Only 243 were made in 1953, and they obviously suited the tycoon who wished to be inconspicuous.

In 1955 and 1956 Chrysler offered their last domestically built Crown Imperial limos. These leviathans of the highway were truly majestic, being built on a wheelbase almost 150 inches long. After 1957 the handful of limos Chrysler offered were semi-customs, hand built in the Ghia plant at Turin, Italy.

Production was very low, thirty-one in 1958 and just sixteen of the 1960 year model. Cadillac certainly outproduced all others in the limo market and they kept production at home. The body style of the 1941 through 1949 series 75 is probably the quintessential limousine. One immediately associates this profile with standing outside of Cartier's or being at dockside at the departure of the *Queen Mary*. It says money,

prestige, elegance, and class as few other motorcars have.

Why have a limo? Owning a 23-foot car and a 20-foot garage will require a compelling argument, I know. Just because they are ostentatious, excessive, and extravagant, would be my reasons.

Actually, until you have driven a postwar series 75 Cadillac, preferably the '47 or '48, you can't imagine the wildly different feel. Some years ago I purchased a 1942 Caddy limo from the back rank of a used-car lot for the sum of $900. It was in lovely condition, and I wheeled it out on the highway with great anticipation.

Sliding around on the black leather seat, I felt as though I had the Twentieth-Century Limited behind me. Turning corners, care must be taken not to climb the curb. That great oversized steering wheel is fine at speed, but turning it to park requires equally great muscles. Every time a sharp curve came up, I thought I was opening the sluice gate at Hoover Dam.

Of course, most limos have full power and do not take a Hercules to drive. The serious objections are their slow, or nonexistent rate of appreciation and the higher cost of repair. Exhaust systems would have to be custom made, for example. On the plus side, limos carry many people and are great for big families. They are usually found in well-preserved condition, if they haven't been ferrying surfers to the beach for ten years.

It would seem a shame if they all disappeared, and we lost this artifact of the time when one class of our society was visible in a very exclusive and distinctive way.

POSTWAR
CAR PROFILES

1946 FORD
SUPER DELUXE
CONVERTIBLE COUPE

Detroit performed a minor miracle in 1942, gradually closing down one auto assembly line after another as they reached the production figure allocated them by the government while their workers shifted quickly into weapons and military-transport production. The transition was made at the height of wage arguments and newly militant union demands, but it went smoothly enough.

Ford fell in line last on the union question, but once that was settled joined every other car maker in drawing up its own victory day plans for a return to auto production. Like General Motors, Ford had recently introduced an all new

A bold, new horizontal grille was the most striking feature of the 1946 Ford.

line and planned to set up that line of models again with only minor cosmetic changes. Ford's new 1946 cars would be 1941 look-alikes, while GM would re-introduce their 1942 line with new grilles.

Ford got off to a flying start, the first 1946 model rolling off the assembly line in July of 1945. They would go on to produce almost 470,000 cars in the model year. The flat head V-8 was still a big draw, and Ford constantly improved it. Piston and ring design were changed, bearings were enlarged, and cooling improved in the postwar version. Styling changes were minimal, being limited to a change in the grille from the vertical bar look of 1942 to a horizontal bar layout in 1946.

In the flush of the postwar spending spree, most buyers didn't care much about price. A creeping wartime inflation had set in leaving the

lowest-cost 1946 model at the price of the top-of-the-line model of 1942. The 1942 line ranged from $830 to $1,193, while the 1946 line started at $1,100 and soared to $2,041. It must be admitted, the glamorous highest-priced model, the woody Sportsman convertible, had no 1942 counterpart.

This Super DeLuxe convertible coupe illustrated here was the only ragtop offered by the River Rouge Company and sold 16,359 units at just under $1,500. Back in 1940, a LaSalle convertible could have been had for just fifty dollars more. The thousand-dollar family car was on its way to oblivion, but as long as wages kept up, no one seemed too alarmed.

This model uses much plastic in its dash, a legacy of the 1940–44 need to conserve zinc and aluminum for the war effort. A tidy, compact model, it was listed as a six-passenger style, but two of those had better be children! The suspension is pure Henry senior, for whom the sun rose and set on traverse semi-elliptic leaf springs. The founder of the company resisted both coil springs and hydraulic brakes longer than any other Detroit car maker. It was a typical Ford irony that the prewar Lincoln Zephyrs, the most aerodynamic cars on the market, had a suspension and braking system more appropriate to a Conestoga covered wagon.

Archaic or not, the suspension works well on this beautiful convertible, with little lean on the curves and virtually no fore and aft pitching. Its weight of 3,240 pounds rides on a 114-inch wheelbase. The V-8 put out exactly 100 horses in 1946, and this delivers more than adequate performance.

Three-quarter view shows a taut, crisply styled convertible, with little overhang on the 114-inch wheelbase.

A beautiful profile. Note the flare out over the rocker panel area, a vestigial reminder of the running board era.

This Ford is surprisingly roomy inside, and the canvas roof provides generous headroom.

Script below headlight identifies this Ford model as a Super DeLuxe.

Taillight detail shows welting is used on light shell as well as on fender.

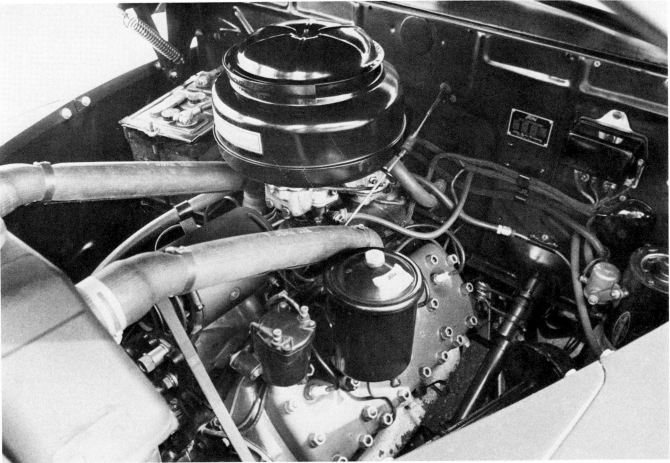

Keith Poyser, the Canton, Ohio, owner of this gem, says it handles very easily and does not convey the feeling of straining he has noted on older 85 horsepower Fords. His car has several sought-after original accessories, such as the floor-button operated Wonder Bar radio and the Ford script spot light. It has obvious appeal to the public and has won Best-in-Show awards.

As might be expected, the Super DeLuxe convertible is among the most popular of all post-war Fords, and despite its relatively high production figure of 16,359, probably no more than a few hundred exists today. Expect to pay $3,000 to $5,000 for a reasonably complete car requiring full restoration. The large number of '46 sedans remaining, and the active effort in Ford reproduction parts, particularly the plastic dash segments, should help facilitate that restoration project.

In the immediate postwar period, only the Sportsman would be a more worthwhile effort. Chances of finding this rare woody are somewhat lower, with total production for 1946–47 at about three thousand units. If you find a 1948 Sportsman, really celebrate, as it will be one of just twenty-eight made that last year for the model.

Other desirable Fords of the period would have to include the slab-sided 1949–51 convertibles and the Custom DeLuxe Victoria two-door hardtop of 1951. The 1955 style is developing a following to rival that of its old competitor, Chevrolet.

Quality lasts, and it is interesting to note that more Fords and Chevys are being restored and driven than any other two makes, a reflection of their continuing popularity with newer generations of car buffs.

In recent years, reproduction parts for this beautiful plastic dash have become available.

The well-proved Ford V-8 produced exactly 100 horsepower in this 1946 edition.

Rear wheel treatment includes a rubber stone shield. Pin striping on the wheels is a carryover from prewar models.

There is no excess trim or ornamentation on this classically simple body style.

1947 PACKARD SUPER CLIPPER EIGHT SEDAN

Most dramatic new designs out of Detroit made the designer well known—famour or infamous, depending on his car's reception in the marketplace. The original Packard Clipper, introduced in April of 1941, has a surprisingly hazy pedigree. Packard stated loftily that it was the product of three of the world's great designers but then declined to name them. Raymond Loewy was the dean of automotive stylists in 1941, but he certainly had nothing to do with this Zephyr-like Packard. In later years, several designers claimed exclusive credit for the Clipper, but this was after the sales race was history and the striking car had become a landmark of

Unmistakably a Packard, the 1947 was a near-identical repeat of the prewar Clipper.

the designer's art. More than likely, every one of the dozen men involved contributed something. The lines werc something like the Darrin Packards, those semi-custom models Howard Darrin crafted to order in his California shop in 1940. Howard Darrin was one of several outside studios Packard President McCauley appealed to for a totally new look.

There is no doubt the Clipper was flawless in shape and seemed a perfect transition from the classic lines of Packard sedans through the thirties, into the newer, more integrated styling. What was equally impressive was the car's engineering and solid performance. The first Clipper continued to use the same straight eight of 282 cubic inches that had served in the 120 line for four or five years but had major improvements in the suspension, including a novel rear sway bar. The interiors were typi-

The Packard pelican, actually a Cormorant, rides gracefully above the classic grille. It was a rarely purchased option in 1947.

The traditional vertical grille is well integrated in the body design, more successfully than with the 1948 style that followed.

cally Packard, low-key luxury, using the finest materials available. Air conditioning was available, as well as a semi-automatic transmission called Electromatic Drive.

The timing of the Clipper launch into the market was unfortunate. First, Packard had spent millions developing a line of cars that totaled forty-one models. Second, they had closed down their in-house body shops and contracted the new model out to Briggs. This well-known company saved Packard money initially but would leave them stranded in the early fifties when Briggs's doors closed for good.

After the war, Packard revived the Clipper series for 1946 and 1947. But Packard then brought out the car that probably had more to do with its eventual demise than any other model. The 1948 looked very much like a 1947 that had overeaten for six months. The svelte lines were now swollen and chubby. The long hood and delicate grille were replaced by a stubby hood over a short and graceless grille. No wonder unflattering names abounded, the most common of which were the "bathtub" and the "pregnant elephant."

Surely a decent facelift on the '47 model could have taken Packard ahead another year or two, giving them time to perfect a superior, all-new model for their anniversary in 1949.

Starting in October of 1945, the re-converted plants started turning out the Clippers, designated as the twenty-first series. When the model run ended in August of 1947, production was just shy of 100,000 cars of all models. What was unusual about the Clipper series was that the same body served the six-cylinder taxicab sedan model as the top-of-the line Custom Super Clipper Eight. The difference came in a lengthened wheelbase (127 inches versus 120 inches) and correspondingly longer front fenders and hood. The eights on the 127-inch platform are, of course, the most graceful looking, and that is the model of choice.

Until ten years ago Packards, along with Lin-

The last, and possibly greatest, classic straight eight engine to power a luxury car, the Super Clipper's would serve through Packard's 1954 model.

coln Zephyrs, were quite low on hobbyists' lists. Now they are coming into their own. If at all possible, hold out for the senior model, as the longer body also carries the best of Packard's postwar engines: the 356-cubic-inch, nine main-bearing straight eight. These cars are in a fluid price state at present. While price guides put this Clipper sedan at $7,000 to $8,000 in perfect condition, it may be difficult to find one that reasonable. A mint example was recently offered at $11,000. Conversely, this writer was recently offered a pair of 1946 Custom Clippers for $1,200. One with a solid, decent body and no engine, the second a parts car with a fine 356 straight eight.

The Packard shown here has an interesting past. As so often happens, a widow finds it difficult to part with a car her late husband prized highly, so it sits unused in a closed garage for many years. The Packard was purchased new in Norwalk, Connecticut. The proud owner died only two years later, and the nearly new Clipper was to sit undisturbed for twenty-three years. It was then sold to a man who found, not surprisingly, that the engine needed attention. In reassembling his handiwork, he inadvertently ignored the numbers stamped on the rod bearing caps. Replaced out of order, they fit poorly; with its valve lifters stuck, he resold the car soon after.

That buyer is still the owner of this lovely machine. In the ten years since acquiring it in Detroit, Greg Olekszak has had little to do beyond repairing the big eight engine. While he

Script prominently says this is a senior series Packard.

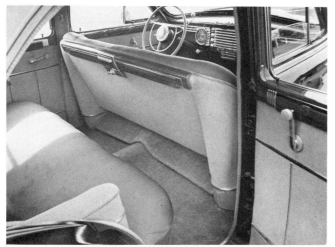

A truly extraordinary find is a low-mileage car with its factory original interior in mint condition. Even the door windlace is unmarred on this car.

Even the Packard crest on the horn ring is as if new on this Super Clipper.

Radios of postwar Packards were living-room size, and the huge speakers provided amazing performance.

Slight bustle back and completely flush taillights preserve the streamlined look of this timeless Packard.

The body proportions on this longer-wheelbase senior series Clipper are perfect. Shorter sheet metal forward of the cowl on the six-cylinder model give it a stubby look.

was putting each rod bearing in its original place, he also replaced the piston rings, though wear on the factory rings was only moderate. Total mileage on the car at that time was 26,000. Only 6,000 additional miles have been put on since then, but Greg is driving the Packard more since joining a new antique car club formed at Goodyear Tire Company's headquarters in Akron, Ohio, where he is employed.

Greg does not believe in babying an old car that is totally restored and safe on the highway. He comments that back before the 55 MPH limit was enacted, he enjoyed passing Cadillacs on turnpike hills. Asked what year Cadillacs, Greg smiles and replies, "Any year."

1948 CHRYSLER TOWN AND COUNTRY CONVERTIBLE COUPE

Like everyone else in Detroit, Chrysler came out of the war with a plant complex totally converted to military production. Their executive board had reached the same decision as Ford's and GM's: re-introduce the 1942 models as soon as the huge task of switching over from tanks and trucks to autos could be managed. Later, while others scrambled to get new postwar designs in the showroom, Chrysler was bemused by the fact that they were selling everything they could make, and put off that new model until 1949. Even then, it was a mild revision of the big, boxy style Chrysler had always favored.

This decision was to have a nearly fatal effect, as each minor styling change saw sales gradually slip away, until the 40 percent drop in 1954 shocked management awake. Virgil Exner then designed a new line of cars for 1955 that literally saved the day and began a new era of up-to-date, competitive Chryslers.

The vehicle we are reviewing here is an unusual example of the big, boxy Chrysler. That, I think, is part of its attraction. With its long hood, split windshield, and massive grille, the Town and Country conveys a pre-war classic car image. It would look right at home in the country club parking lot nestled between a 1941 Packard and a 1937 Pierce Arrow.

Wooden bodied station wagons were a popular body style in prewar America. A cross between a sedan and a truck, they performed a wide range of hauling chores. In the postwar period several makers would continue to offer them, with their wood content gradually diminishing until they became all metal in the mid fifties.

A truly massive sculptured look was in vogue in the forties. Twin gooseneck mirrors were original accessories.

Profile view of the T & C shows how well wood and steel were incorporated into a smooth, flowing line.

Stern view reveals huge deck lid. Two powerful spring-loaded cylinders are employed to ease its operation.

Beautiful attention to detail is evident in the massive ash doors. The striated mahogany in this 1948 edition is now simulated in Di-Noc film, proven more durable than the earlier wood veneer.

The Town and Country concept was something quite different. From the beginning the idea was to build a *structure* of wood, not a metal body merely decorated with wood. The production cost differential between these two methods was enormous, and eventually Chrysler would end up putting their prized "Town and Country" script on a vinyl-sided convertible in 1968. But in that period between 1941 and 1950, the market was such that thousands of people were willing to pay the premium, and master craftsmen turned out the beautiful sedans and convertibles in large numbers.

First conceived as a sedan, the '41 Town and Country was based on the seven-passenger, long wheelbase platform. By 1946, the latest shorter version was produced on the production line of the Jefferson Avenue plant in Detroit. Here the massive doors were hung and the heavy wooden-framed trunk lids secured to each body. You would have to travel to a small town in Arkansas to appreciate the expense of making these gleaming ash components. In the vast plant of the Pekin Wood Company in Helena, Arkansas, craftsmen skillfully created the furniture that would become a car. These units were carefully boxed and shipped to Detroit, where metal components were added, such as hinges and the steel panels to hold window glass in each door.

The two-tone effect of the wooden surfaces was striking, with framing members of ash, varnished exactly like the exposed wood of a speedboat. The recessed steel panels were covered with Honduras mahogany veneer. These were subject to splitting if not carefully maintained, so Di-Noc, a synthetic wood grain material used on auto dashboards, was employed after late 1947.

The golden age of the Town and Country is the period between 1946 and 1949. The early sedan-wagon of 1941 and 1942 is rare and the 1950 T & C Newport is a beauty, but those in the middle years were the supreme effort.

The sedan was based on the Windsor series

The hood crest sports a red crown and the traditional Chrysler seal.

A well-finished interior with a passenger-controlled light over the seat.

Monumental chrome hinges were a must for the very heavy trunk lid.

While the dash of the T & C is refined, its flamboyant radio is almost jukebox size.

and had a shorter wheelbase than the convertible, which was based on the New Yorker. Just under 4,000 pounds, the sedan was powered by the venerable "Spitfire" six. Though rated at only 114 horses, this six moves the heavy sedan along quite crisply, the deliberate shifting provided by the semi-automatic Fluid Drive. There is one sleeper among the sedans, and that is the C-39 of 1946. That year only, Chrysler made just 100 straight eight editions on the 127.5-inch New Yorker chassis. Less than half a dozen are known to exist, and I foolishly passed up the chance to obtain one ten years ago, declining the car at a reasonable price because virtually all the wood was beyond restoration. This is a serious factor to consider today. The one estimate I obtained recently on a total replacement of a convertible's wood was $4,000, and that, of course, did not include installing it. I recently examined a nice original 1947 T & C sedan at a car show. It

had been "ruined," in the opinion of several Chrysler experts present, because the owner had antiqued the wood. This noxious material hides the glorious grain of the ash and cannot be removed easily.

Considering the incredible amount of skilled hand work on each car, the original prices seem very low. The sedan was under $3,000, and the gorgeous convertible sold for $3,200—just $1,200 more than a '47 Studebaker coupe. Assembling the convertible was such a tedious and time-consuming job, it was done on a stationary line. Only the postwar Lincoln Continental enjoyed that luxury among other makers.

This beautiful Town and Country convertible is owned by Robert Dierksheide of Findlay, Ohio. Bob is a devoted Chrysler fan and has, among a dozen other Mopars, the matching showpiece sedan to his convertible. He has found that the T & C will draw the largest crowd at car meets and the most applause in parades. Without question, these relatively low-production cars improved Chrysler's image in the postwar period more than any other car until the mighty "300" came along.

An enthusiast, I will venture to say that the Town and Country is one of the very few postwar cars that successfully combined the elegance and craftsmanship of the classic car era with the comfort and roadability of the modern auto. I think it has unlimited potential for dollar appreciation, and would not be at all surprised to see prime examples near the forty- or fifty-thousand-dollar range in the next decade. Thus the greater difficulty in effecting a restoration should not deter one from the effort. Fortunately, vast quantities of mechanical parts and trim are available, due to the large production of standard Windsor and New Yorker models.

Mr. Dierksheide bought his convertible back in 1977. Its mechanical condition was questionable, but most of the wood was very solid and unmarred. Accompanied by the family station wagon, Bob attempted to drive the car home from New Jersey. He labored along until the generator quit. The wisdom of carrying a tow

Mr Dierkesheide does not plan to be caught short of parts for his forties Chryslers.

The owner believes this decayed Town & Country convertible, stored with his parts cars, could be restored.

The L-head straight eight developed 135 horsepower and was the standard powerplant of the New Yorker series, of which the Town & Country was a top-of-the-line sub-series.

bar was confirmed, and the family wagon towed the T & C home to Findlay.

A full restoration followed, and there is not an inch on this beauty that does not rate a top score. Some colors don't go well with wood, but here Noel green—a correct, original color—is most attractive with the two-tone wood.

To see how the auto scene has changed, one has only to inspect closely the current Town and Country "gas saver" from Chrysler and to compare it with this motorcar. One is "cost-effective," the other is craftsmanship at its peak. Robots can assemble vehicles, but only loving care and consummate skill could create this 1948 Chrysler Town and Country.

1948 OLDSMOBILE FUTURAMIC 98 CONVERTIBLE COUPE

Since the demise of the Studebaker in 1966, Oldsmobile has been the oldest American wheeled-goods producer in continuous operation. Ranson E. Olds was assembling cars in 1897, having built an experimental steamer ten years before. Although he left the Olds Motor Works in 1904, General Motors kept his name when they absorbed that company in 1908.

Postwar Olds of 1946 and 1947 carried the pontoon fender styling of the GM prestige leader, Cadillac. They sold well as car-starved Americans literally kept overnight vigils at every maker's showrooms when new models were due. Steel shortages and crippling strikes were the main problems as labor and management strove

to come to terms after the war. To help meet demand, General Motors was assembling Buicks, Olds, and Pontiacs on the same line at several plants.

The first distinctive Olds of the postwar era was timed for the division's golden anniversary in 1948. Gone were the free-standing fenders, replaced by the smooth, rounded shape of the future. Hence, the name, Futuramic. The hood was lower, and the windshield 30 percent larger. The car was 14 inches wider than it was high, whereas prewar cars were more nearly one-to-one in ratio. Hydra-Matic was a valued option, coming several years before Studebaker, Packard, or Hudson could offer an automatic gear shifter. Oddly enough, not all Olds had the new styling. Four lower-priced lines—the 66, 68, 76, and 78 series—still carried the now obsolete bodies of 1946 and 1947.

Stylist Harley Earl's new look was an imme-

Ultra-simple grille and a split windshield are notable features of the 1948 senior series Olds.

diate success, and the 98 was not only the price leader but also the sales leader. The big, 4,035-pound convertible was popular: nearly 13,000 were sold. It had two archaic features. Under the hood for its last year was the venerable straight eight, displacing a modest 257 cubic inches and producing just 115 horsepower at 3,600 RPM. The second holdover was the use of 16-inch rims. These 6.50-by-16 tires would be replaced in 1949 by modern 7.10-by-15 low-pressure tires. The car has a wheelbase of 125 inches and measures just 213 inches in length. The 98 convertible listed for $2,624 in 1948. Its performance was greatly improved in 1949, when for $200 more, one could enjoy the potent new Rocket 88 V-8 engine.

The fine example of this rare convertible illustrated here is a joint restoration by a father-and-son team, David and Dell Moell of Richfield, Ohio. They located their car in Akron, Ohio, through a newspaper ad in 1978. It had been through many hands but had spent most of its thirty years in California and Oklahoma.

Deciding on a frame-up restoration, they sent the basically sound hood, deck lid, and fenders out for sandblasting. Unfortunately, both deck lid and hood were ruined—stretched and warped by a cleaning technique that was incorrect for the metal. The owners were lucky to find replacements and even located two N.O.S. front fenders.

Well into their project, the Moells realized the straight eight did not have the exact specifications the shop manual called for. One of the car's many previous owners apparently had replaced the original engine with a prewar Pontiac block.

All convertibles look their best with the top down, and this Olds is no exception.

Driver's view on getting into the Olds. Steering wheel position is high, typical of the period.

Smooth lines of the rear fender are worthy of a closeup look. Note the chrome trim that sets off the fuel cap.

Front-fender styling carries through to meet the projecting rear fender. Chrome trim is low key and functional.

The passenger compartment is unusually large on this 98 Futuramic. Note how the canvas top extends beyond the rear axle.

Due for replacement, this was not the original GM
factory block, though of the same period.

A restored, authentic steering wheel sets off a
gleaming dash on the completed car.

Here is the car as found. It had been dechromed but not substantially altered.

Part-way through the project, the restored body has been mounted on the chassis.

The dash and steering wheel looked like this the day the car was purchased.

They found an engine with the correct specifications and are rebuilding it for future installation.

The car had been dechromed, so the Moclls have had to search for the missing trim. Some original dash pieces will be replaced by new old-stock as soon as they can be found.

Oldsmobile sedans of the period prior to these with the Rocket 88 engine are not as popular as the newer models. The convertible is, however, among the most sought after of GM's postwar cars. What is strange is that the 1949 and 1950 Futuramic converts with the great V-8 usually bring a few thousand dollars *less* than the 1948 with its modest straight eight. Perhaps it is because so many car buffs associate the V-8 engine with today's autos and the long straight eight with the classic-car era.

1949 STUDEBAKER CHAMPION TWO-DOOR SEDAN

Studebaker's great achievements over the years, and they were many and substantial, were possible because the company was small enough and flexible enough to move fast when opportunity knocked. Specifically, their "approval route" was probably one-quarter the torturous length of General Motors' route. Before deciding what to do, GM might spend months deciding which division would do it.

Studebaker finished financially strong after V-J Day, having built thousands of army trucks, aircraft engines, and the remarkable Weasels. (A tracked snow cruiser, the Weasel was so well built that a local army surplus dealer recently imported sixty like-new units—surplus from Norwegian army-transport stores.)

The company was still getting bouquets for the peppy and sturdy "Champion" that had sold so well in 1939 and 1940. Like most of the competition, after the war Stude put their old 1942 dies and jigs in place and offered the same cars in 1946.

But their 1947 model surprised both Detroit and the country: They leapfrogged the next ten years of creeping evolution and design and changed the shape of all cars to come.

While styling traces of fenders remained, the car was now a lower, wider box with the first full-width grille (possibly excepting that of the 1942 Caddy)—incorporating the fenders and hood and integrating the bumper into a unified front end. The striking, practical result was to turn the cramped, five-passenger prewar car into a roomy six-passenger model. Seats were now

Profile view of the then-radical Studebaker. Short hood and large doors were practical elements that made for more interior space and easy access.

actually in the space that had heretofore been *outside* the doors, space wasted between the front and rear fenders. Seven inches lower than the now-dated 1946 model, the car handled much better. Gaining 10 inches in rear-seat width and 6 inches up front, the car was still only 69 inches wide. One had to wonder why this common-sense method of increasing interior space hadn't yet been tried. If you study design trends up to 1940, you will note that fender shape, length, and decoration gives a car its identity. (Stylists could no more give up fenders than they cared to give up the long hood when engineers told them they could tuck the engine in the trunk and drive through the rear wheels directly.) Studebaker dared to build this new design concept across their full line, gambling that the public would like it. The gamble paid off and caused some embarrassment in certain of Detroit's boardrooms.

The management team then in place was one of the strongest they would ever have. Virgil Exner and Bob Rourke on the design side; Raymond Loewy the outside style contributor; Roy Cole, Gene Hardig, George Matthews, and Perry Sullivan covering all phases of engineering.

Quality control was extremely high at their South Bend plant, and it is not unusual to find '47 and '48 models in the barn today with original paint that still gleams. Once the country got over joking about the car that looked like it was coming when it was actually going, the solid merit of the new look sunk in. Studebaker then enjoyed their best years ever, culminating in sales of over one-quarter of a million cars in 1950—their all-time record.

Floyd Clymer was the dean of auto writers in the late 1940s. He waited in line for seven

Rear view that led many to ask, "Is it coming or going?"

Three-quarter view is pleasing and contemporary even today, nearly four decades after it was first sketched.

This grille was the last for the original sheet metal of the 1947 line. A major facelift forward of the cowl would be done in 1950.

Engine room of the tiny flat-head six has not been detailed on this car. Strange accessory at left is a siren, memento of a previous owner.

Rear-seat passengers were flooded with light, though vision to the side was no better than in conventional cars. Arm rests doubled as storage compartments on this model of the 1950 Studebaker coupe.

Raymond Loewy believed that simple could be beautiful—witness this spare but attractive dash.

The wide-angle camera lens only slightly exaggerates the dramatic bullet nose of the 1950 version of the postwar Studebakers.

months, like everyone else, to plunk down his $1,987.42 and take delivery of a Champion DeLuxe five-passenger coupe. He then drove his Stude on a punishing westward trip, interviewing hundreds of other Studebaker owners along the way. Paying thirty-one cents per gallon for his gas, Mr. Clymer finally covered over five thousand miles in his new Champion. The overdrive-equipped model delivered 18 MPG in traffic and 26 MPG on the open highway.

He surveyed five thousand new-model owners and of the three thousand who replied, fewer than 6 percent rated the car as fair or poor. While the overwhelming majority were delighted with the Studebakers, they were not immune to the "sticker shock" that existed even then. Most Americans were accustomed to family cars in the $600 to $1,000 range before World War II, and 12 percent of the survey respondents thought the new Studebakers were overpriced at an average cost of $2,000.

The 1949 Champion featured is the last model of the new postwar design before the first major "bullet-nose" facelift of 1950. Garlton Adams of Westlake, Ohio, purchased the car in 1964 as a clean original with about 70,000 miles on it and has added about 10,000 mostly summertime miles. He particularly likes two of Studebaker's more famous options: the hill-holder and the overdrive unit. The patented hill-holder device enables a driver stopped on a steep incline to move off smoothly without stalling the engine. The overdrive drops engine RPMs once at cruising speed (over 35 MPH), thus saving both fuel and engine wear. It is a feature being revived in today's cars.

Mr. Adams's association with Studebakers goes back a long time. In 1934, his father gave him a 1927 Studebaker roadster for his eighteenth birthday. The family car was a big 1930 President sedan with sidemounts. He had owned several others over the years, but currently is driving and restoring the 1949 shown and a 1950 Starlite coupe.

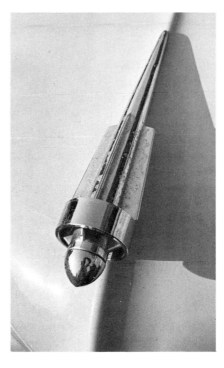

Rocketlike hood ornament graces the nose of the Champion line.

From 1947 to 1952, the most unusual model of the Studebaker line was undoubtedly the Starlight coupe, with its wraparound rear glass treatment. This is a 1950 edition.

Even by today's standards, this Champion is modest in power. The flat-head six displaces 169 cubic inches and produces 80 horsepower at 4,000 RPM. It uses a one-barrel Carter carburetor. Mr. Adams's studebaker cost $1,657 in 1949 and weighs just 2,720 pounds. With over 80,000 miles on it, gas mileage is 25 MPG in town and nearly 30 MPG on the turnpike. Needless to say, Mr. Adams sees no reason to turn it in for anything newer.

1951 CHRYSLER NEW YORKER DELUXE CONVERTIBLE COUPE

Had you asked the average American to evaluate Chrysler around 1950, you might have gotten an answer something like this: "Engineering always first rate. Bodies always sort of big and boxy. They made some kind of weird car back in the thirties that never caught on, think they called it the 'Airflow.'"

Like most of Detroit, Chrysler didn't make a major styling change for several years after the war—not until the company's 25th Anniversary in 1949. Unfortunately, that change was a subtle, transitional one that might have worked for a year or two but didn't have what was needed for the next five years, the time they retained it.

On the long wheelbase New Yorker chassis, and powered by the new hemi engine, this convertible is a knockout from any angle.

What did help was the introduction of the legendary "hemi" engine in the senior Chrysler line of 1951. The ancient and reliable straight eight was gone, and a really new overhead V-8 sat under the hood of the gleaming New Yorkers and Imperials.

The major innovation that set this engine apart from other modern V-8s was the shape of its combustion chamber. The spark plug was placed directly in the center of a hemispherical chamber, meaning the time required for combustion was reduced and the engine's ability to use that higher heat energy was increased. It could accomplish this well even on regular fuel, not requiring premium as did other big V-8s from GM. It also ran seemingly forever giving scarcely any cause for concern about carbon formation, and it incorporated a highly efficient cooling system that completely surrounded the valve parts, making for long life.

The engine was not cheap to build (and cost was finally one of the reasons for its replacement in the 1959 line) as it required twin rocker arm shafts. Management, however, knew this engine had enormous growth possibilities and considered the added cost was justified.

The public was also swayed (not one hopes, literally) by the new Oriflow shock absorbers. They gave the 4,000-pound-plus sedans the edge in road holding, and that other dramatic innovation, power steering, allowed any driver to steer and park the big Chrysler with ease. All in all, 1951 was a year of considerable accomplishment. The bouquets were not long in arriving: *Motor Trend* magazine made Chrysler the "Car of the Year." *Consumer Reports*, an organization some car buffs suspect had a bias against big, heavy cars, lauded the new model. Then that crustiest of car lovers and critics, Floyd Clymer, wrote in *Popular Mechanics:* "I abused it. . . . I couldn't make it leak, heat, squeak or rattle. It responded to every conceivable kind of test and came through with flying colors."

Chrysler's unique Fluid-Torque drive was used on the New Yorkers, which rode on the long wheelbase of 131.5 inches. The "hemi" engine in the New Yorker convertible has a displacement of 331 cubic inches and produces 180 horsepower. Production of this larger series convert was 2,200 units, half that of the less expensive Windsor series model. These figures include both 1951 and the virtually identical models made through November of 1952.

The solid engineering contributions of 1951 may have obscured the two vital factors Chrysler needed if they hoped to place and stay in the "top ten" (they had been there briefly in 1952): a top-rank stylist and a fully automatic transmission. They had the latter in all lines in 1954, and the former in the person of Virgil Exner— whose stunning 1955 "hundred-million-dollar-look" line many credit with saving a failing company.

Bob Porter of Cleveland, Ohio, restored the

The "carved-in-metal" look was king in 1951, and this front end typifies the designer's interest in the car as rolling sculpture.

Rear view of the big New Yorker. The four light fixtures are almost square in shape, in keeping with a design that does not pretend to be streamlined.

Chrysler stylists were masters at rounding off the box. The gravel shield and fender moulding are beautifully executed, and even the gas cap is used as a style element.

Not a monument to chrome, just the center pier of the massive grille this Chrysler wears.

Twin spotlights top off this restoration. Exact reproductions are marketed today, with all correct car plates available.

Chrysler favored crowns and wings for their badges. This is the attractive hood ornament all New Yorkers wore in 1951.

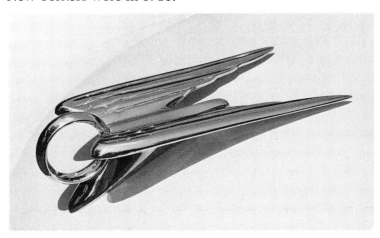

Detail of the driver's view. Fluid torque drive was a popular, trouble-free semi-automatic that Chrysler used throughout their products.

The 1951 Chrysler dash was a beauty with all the vital indicators directly before the driver. The perfect steering wheel came from a parts sedan.

big convertible shown here, resisting the temptation to duplicate the one selected in 1951 as the Indianapolis Memorial Day Classic pace car.

The car had turned the century mark on its odometer when Mr. Porter purchased it some three years ago. Despite living in Cleveland, the salt capital of the world, since 1953, the body was essentially sound. Ten years of dead storage in dry quarters helped, undoubtedly. The car must have been a southern or western model initially since it has never had a heater mounted.

The car was complete, but its engine was in poor condition. Rather than rebuild, Bob purchased a sound '51 sedan showing 56,000 miles

The legendary "hemi" in its introductory version displaces 331 cubic inches and produces 180 horsepower.

Chrysler featured this Highlander plaid for several years. Note the well-fitted boot on this carefully restored convertible.

with both a fine engine and an excellent interior. The sedan's mint steering wheel and several dash instruments were also switched to the convertible. At $300, this was a sound investment and proves the value of a parts car in any difficult restoration. The original fluid drive works well but required a new governor switch. The front end was rebuilt with new old-stock parts and all chrome redone.

The car is painted its original color, a daffodil yellow. While many hobbyists grow increasingly uneasy the farther from home they drive their prized restorations, Mr. Porter has put over 10,000 miles on his New Yorker—including a Sunbelt run from Cleveland to Atlanta, Georgia—with no difficulty.

1951 CADILLAC SERIES 62 CONVERTIBLE COUPE

Cadillac and Packard vied for leadership of the luxury-car market until the beginning of the fifties. Both the Packard Company and the top GM Division had come out of the war with a record of brilliant engineering accomplishments. How quickly they would adapt those skills to the market of the new-car showroom would make the difference. Packard would produce torsion-level suspension, a great new V-8, and its own automatic transmission. Unfortunately, their engineering achievements lagged behind those of Cadillac, which had the modern V-8 in 1949 and the Hydra-Matic as early as 1941.

Packard had what some experts called the most recognizable grille in the world, until 1948.

In the estate setting it was created for, this 1951 Cadillac appears right at home. The fake air scoop at the rear fender is a striking styling touch.

Then their stylists floundered while struggling to keep the recognition of a vertical grille on cars that were rapidly being styled on the horizontal. In 1951 the last major new Packard body style was introduced, and continuity with the past seemed dim if not lost. Cadillac, on the other hand, somehow has managed to retain a family look from 1941 to the present. The dome-shaped hood and a broad, egg-crate grille have been common factors over the years despite many variations.

While the slab-sided designs of Kaiser, Studebaker, and Ford were selling, Cadillac elected to retain vestigial shapes of fenders, and hoods that still reflected the engine beneath them. One of their promises was that they would never leave last year's customer too far behind. How did the buyer of a 1950 Packard feel when he saw the radically different 1951 line? Certainly his model became obsolete more rapidly, painful both to the ego and the wallet.

The Cadillac "eggcrate" grille was bold and attractive in 1951 with the hood "V" insuring instant identification.

Smooth, rounded lines were popular in 1951, and the taillights could not yet be classified as fins.

Cadillac proudly proclaimed their car the "Standard of the World" and could point to a string of great achievements, from the Dewar trophy of 1908 through the mighty V-16 of 1930. But so could other makes. Packard, Pierce Arrow, and Peerless had enjoyed being the choice of the wealthy and discriminating for decades. What seemed to make the difference at Cadillac was the depth of coporate talent available. Their engineering staff of the fifties reads like a who's who of that profession, and they were early to recognize the importance of color and style in auto sales. The control over the final product that stylist designers such as Bill Mitchell exercised was not to be found anywhere else, except during Raymond Loewy's years with Studebaker.

The 1951 convertible shown here is a refinement of a body new in 1950. The one-piece curved windshield is the first for Cadillac, while the vertical dummy air intake was a carryover. What had been modest bumper guards grew to large bullet-shaped units on the 1951 models. (These would continue to grow until on the '55 they were nearly obscene and a real hazard to slow-moving pedestrians.) Although sales climbed to over 110,000 only six thousand customers sought out the convertible. The car weighed 4,316 pounds, rode on a wheelbase of 126 inches, and took up 216 inches in the family garage. It cost almost $4,000, or about $1,200 more than a DeSoto convertible of the same year.

These early fifties Cadillacs, hard to fault when new, are even harder to fault today. The overhead valve V-8 of 331 cubic inches mated to the smooth-shifting Hydra-Matic are a perfect pair. The quality of materials, chrome, paint, fabric or leather, the fit, and the finish are superb. I recently inspected a 1951 Coupe de Ville, in stunning condition, and was told by the proud original owner that it was not restored but original. Even with meticulous care, not many of Detroit's products still appear as new as the one shown here after three decades.

Cadillac ads pushed quality and that "Great Master High-Compression Engine."

Though highly stylized, this hood ornament is still recognizable as the traditional winged goddess.

Cadillac crest and "V" emblem have been on every model made since the war, in one form or another.

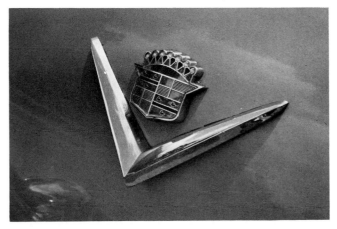

Ready to take the owner to distant places, Cadillac in 1951 was refined and elegant.

In recent years, the cachet of "Body by Fleetwood" has given way to "Interior by Fleetwood" as all GM bodies are Fisher Division products.

Press in on the jewel reflector, and the whole light unit tilts open to gain access to the gas tank.

This 1951 light-blue beauty is the proud possession of Jack Schoonover of Canton, Ohio. He plans further work to improve its cosmetic appearance, such as locating new wheel-cover medallions. When he purchased the car a few years ago, the interior had been redone. The narrow pleats do not follow the original, which were wider. Riding in the car with the top up gives no hint of its being a convertible. The well-fitted canvas does not slap or complain. Mr. Schoonover has driven the car from Canton, Ohio, to Pontiac, Michigan, and reports it was a relaxing experience.

Obviously, the convertible is the car of choice for the fifties shopper who gets bitten by the Cadillac bug. You should expect to pay from $2,500 to $5,000 for an unrestored convert

A relatively spartan dash for a luxury car. The owner is seeking a mint shift lever knob to finish this restoration.

The tire design is not authentic, but the wire wheel covers are correct and original.

Where do you find a 1951 Caddy? This one was for sale recently. Offered at $2,500, as is, requiring full restoration. When finished, its value would range from $10,000 on up.

needing extensive work. Beauties like the one shown may run from $10,000 to $17,000 or more.

However, the gorgeous Coupe de Ville is a fine second choice. From 1950 thru 1953 the same sleek, rounded look prevailed, before the squared-off, massive, and bulky look of the later fifties appeared. The coupe will be less expensive, and of course the standard sedans may be found as low as a few thousand dollars.

Cadillac would soon enter a period of rather bizarre flamboyance from 1958 to 1960, but the elegant and restrained models of the early fifties were truly the "Standard of the World."

1951 HUDSON HORNET SEDAN

Hudson, opening their doors in 1909, was one of Detroit's early pioneers. They built solid, middle-class cars that managed to find a small, secure niche in the marketplace up to World War II. After peace came, they continued to market their modestly streamlined autos of prewar designs in equally modest numbers.

When the showroom banners went up for the 1948 models, however, the public could not believe the cars awaiting them. Staid, conservative Hudson had produced a fastback family sedan of style and comfort that could outrace almost every other stock car around. For the first time, body and frame were totally unitized by thousands of welds—'totally' in that the curv-

Even today, the Hudson looks daringly different. Vision from inside the car is good despite the high belt line and shallow windows.

ing box beam girders actually ran *outside* the rear wheels, providing enormous strength and impact protection to the car's sides. Its floor below the side rails, the "Monobilt Body" was quickly dubbed the "step-down" Hudson by publicists.

This surprising feat was accomplished by one of the most talented engineering staffs in Detroit. Hudson buffs know well the names of Frank Spring, Stuart Baits, and Reid Railton and marvel at what they accomplished in a six-cylinder family car. In the next six years the step-down Hudson was to become a legend on nearly every race track in the country. Without going into a detailed list here, suffice it to say that the Hudson not only beat all domestic competition in its day but defeated Porsches and Jaguars in the International 500. Even today, a few thirty-year-old specimens are raced, where rules permit their running, and frequently win.

Sculptured crease lines along the sides repeat the body line and serve to bring the rear end down.

Bumper and grille were styled as one. Some critics thought the triangle shape had an unfortunate resemblance to a towbar.

Driver's view of the Hudson Hornet dash. Note the unusual single-digit speedometer at the left.

In 1948, Hudson introduced the "step-down" Monobuilt sedan. It was an immediate success.

This factory art graphically explains the novel body-frame method of construction. The sturdy box was highly resistant to flexing under the worst road conditions.

Projectile-shaped hood ornament repeats the triangle theme of the grille on the big Hornet.

How was this possible in a tanklike, 4,000 pound, six-passenger car? First, the lowest center of gravity of any then-current Detroit car, with similar ground clearance. Second, the most rigid, non-flexing, body frame around. Third, suspension that would be advanced today, with anti-sway bars front and rear and Hudson's unique splayed-out spring system. Add to these factors the swift response of dual carbs and super precise center-point steering and you have a beautifully upholstered racing machine.

The original car and engine were honed and perfected, and a new version was offered in 1951 as the Hornet. The L-head six had been revamped and fitted with a high-compression aluminum head. Now at 308 cubic inches, the sturdy six produced 145 horsepower at 3,800 RPM.

It is this car we feature, owned by Dwayne Stone of Marietta, Ohio.

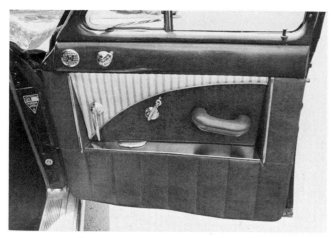

Fortunate the owner who finds a car with this flawless an interior. Now thirty-two years old, this door panel looks nearly new.

The rear window seems reversed on this Hudson, possibly to provide a stronger roof pillar. Compare these lines with the 1984 Thunderbird. Both designers came to a similar conclusion.

Mr. Stone purchased the car in 1981 and has been able to trace it back through four owners to its original sale in 1951. A professional chauffeur purchased it out of the showroom in Sandusky, Ohio, as a fiftieth wedding anniversary gift to his wife. Some years later, after his death, his widow sold it. The new owner and his brother restored it to running condition and put only a thousand miles on the car in seven years.

In 1977 the fourth owner took the car to Columbus, Ohio, still showing just 12,225 miles on the odometer. In 1980 a retired Hudson mechanic completely overhauled the somewhat neglected engine, and all accessories were rebuilt or replaced. This owner used the car more extensively and ran the odometer up to 19,000 miles, at which point he sold it to Mr. Stone.

Mr. Stone was not partial to the original black finish, so the car was redone in dark blue. All stainless and chrome trim was removed and buffed or replated. The present owner has wisely preserved the near mint original interior. Only the driver's seat shows wear, and difficulty in locating a yard of original material is delaying that repair.

Mr. Stone owns several other postwar cars, including a 1948 Lincoln Continental and a 1953 Buick Roadmaster. He rates the Hudson a delightful road car with more power and torque than he expected of a six-cylinder engine. He finds the deliberate shifts of the early Hydra-Matic a little different than his Buick's Dynaflow.

He remarks, as does everyone who studies the car closeup, at the sheer quality of its construction. As a former Hudson engineer once observed mournfully to the author: "They just couldn't break that damn habit of over-building everything!" Unable to finance a totally new car for 1955, the step-down design was old hat to a fickle public after a seven-year run, and the 1954 facelift was its last gasp. In May of that year, Hudson ceased to exist. Cars wearing the Hud-

The chrome alloy block, four main-bearing six that ruled the stock car race circuit for a decade, this L-head engine developed 145 horses in the 1951 edition.

The biggest rear-seat arm rest ever made graces the original interior of this Hornet.

Hudson proudly put this tag on the door post of every car, identifying their unique method of construction.

son name would roll from the Kenosha, Wisconsin assembly line of American Motors until 1957, but true Hudsonites equate these Nash hybrids with the "Packabakers" of that firm's last days. Looking at the racing records of the early fifties, one has to agree that Hudson went out in a blaze of glory.

All the step-down designs are collectible, but the Hollywood two-door hardtop and the low production brougham convertible are scarce and desirable.

1953 OLDSMOBILE SUPER 88 HOLIDAY COUPE

In its fourth year, Olds was riding the wave of popularity it had attained after introducing the potent Rocket engine in the 88 series. Just above the base line in that series, Olds offered a choice of five Super 88s. These were among the most powerful mid-priced cars you could drive off the showroom floor. In 1953 the Rocket engine was putting out 165 horses in the Super 88. Only the limited production Fiesta luxury convertible offered more in an Olds—and that, just five additional horses. Power was selling family cars in the early fifties, and makes like Studebaker with much smaller V-8s in their largest models suffered accordingly.

Hydra-Matic was a $132 option, but the automatic found on our subject car is not the nor-

The Olds look in 1953 is becoming massive. A gravel shield is employed, though no separate fender exists as such.

mal Olds unit. In 1953, GM had just completed a giant new transmission plant when it was totally destroyed by fire. In the flurry of stopgap solutions to the problems that ensued, Buick Dynaflow transmissions were hastily adapted for other GM family cars. Cadillac used some, and Olds used many, including the one in the car shown here.

Olds dominated NASCAR racing in the early fifties, with the step-down Hudsons their most formidable adversary. Later in the decade, Chrysler launched the hemi engine and took the racing headlines.

The light, lean, and powerful cars of 1950 and 1951 gradually grew heavier—directed more to the Buick Roadmaster and Lincoln Capri customer. The Super 88 Holiday coupe is such a car. Wire-spoke wheelcovers and fender skirts were added for a sporty look. The stylists put stainless bows in the roof for the feel of a con-

Nose-on view shows a downward sweep to bumper and grille that make the car seem to hug the road.

Wire wheel covers and rear fender skirts add a sporty touch to this Holiday hardtop.

90

vertible. The truly massive grille and front bumper were for blatant luxury. Whatever we may think of this package today, it hit the target in 1953. Over 34,000 of this Holiday coupe were sold. Compared with the excesses of all Detroit in the later fifties, the '53 Olds is restrained in style.

This particular Holiday is almost totally original, having had just three owners and indicating a total of 82,000 miles. Dr. Herbert Mahler of Findlay, Ohio, spotted the car for sale in 1973 on a trip to Virginia. An Olds mechanic in Winchester had given it loving care for many years. Dr. Mahler drove it home with little difficulty, and since then the car has required only a rebuild of that alien Dynaflow transmission. The Mahler family likes the Olds because it starts at the first turn of the key in any weather, offers a comfortable ride, and still delivers about 16 MPG.

Chrome ribs across the headliner stimulate the bows of a true convertible top, a popular ploy in the early days of hardtop design.

The 1953 Olds still retains a family resemblance to the 1948 Futuramic seen earlier in this book.

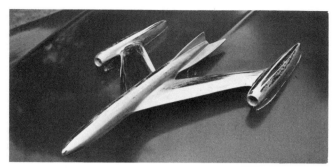

The Rocket 88 has, logically enough, a rocket ship on its hood leading the way.

Ornamentation on this Olds is highly detailed, with an elaborate globe set in a chrome ring featured on the hood.

A rather conservative dash layout locates the clock at the extreme right side.

Olds in the postwar years provides a long list of desirable cars. Naturally, convertibles are up at the top and available in many models. Among the still low priced big series are the 1959 Super 88 and 98 open cars. With less chrome trim than the bedecked '58s, they may still be found in restorable condition in the $2,000 range. The Starfire series from 1961 to 1966 was offered as both super luxury coupe and convertible. The 1964 convertible and the striking 1965 closed hardtop coupe are personal favorites. The closed-model Starfires do not have the following of certain Chevy and Ford models. Therefore, prices ranging from $500 to $1,000 are still seen, which represent remarkable value. You might also be intrigued by the compact series introduced in 1961: the F85. These are delightful cars, especially the hardtops and convertibles. They were powered by their exclusive engine, a high-tech aluminum V-8 of 215 cubic inches. The rare find would be the Jetfire coupe of 1963, which introduced turbo charging to the compact car. Parts, especially in the drivetrain, may be a problem for these Olds.

The first successful postwar front wheel drive automobile in America can't be overlooked either. The Toronado fastback coupe of 1966 was a styling and engineering tour de force winning several prestigious awards. Production reached 40,000, so they are reasonably plentiful eighteen years later. More recent models will not have as much appeal as those of the first two years—as with Cadillacs' FWD Eldorado, introduced in 1967.

Cutlass has been among America's most popular cars since the late sixties. A collector will want to bone up on the various 4–4–2 sports versions offered from 1964 through 1971.

Parts availability on most postwar Oldsmobiles is generally good, as with any make that had an annual production of usually more than a half million units, and that has a very active national club.

This Olds is a "driver," and restoration has not yet included detailing the engine compartment. The OHV V-8 produces 165 horsepower.

The same globe device featured on the hood floats here in a block of plastic incorporated into the attractive steering wheel.

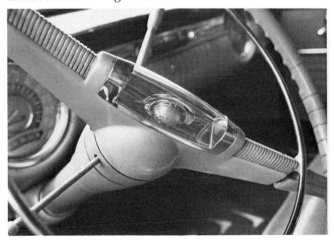

1953 BUICK ROADMASTER 76-C CONVERTIBLE COUPE

I n 1942, Buick had gone into war production, and temporarily out of the car business, with an impressive array of successful cars to its credit. From the bold new models of 1936 to the rakish, streamlined models of 1942, Buick sold all they could make. The "valve-in-head" straight eight was a fine engine and would serve for sixteen years—until the debut of the modern V-8 featured here.

Buick sales prospered through the shake out years when the independents were having problems. One reason was the introduction of the Dynaflow transmission in 1948. The public had only Hydra-Matic to compare it with and found this definitely smoother. Early Hydra-Matic units let you know with a noticeable thump as

Compare this view to the frontispiece car in the barn. Not the same car, it is, however, the identical model: the very desirable Buick 76-C Roadmaster convertible.

each of its four shifts were made. Dynaflow had a torque convertor unit that made shifting a seemingly continuous, imperceptible event. The public didn't seem to mind the loss of some power and the far-from-blinding acceleration.

By 1952, Buick had a solid lock on fourth-place ranking in sales, industry wide. Despite a major strike that caused a widespread steel shortage, Buick sold 321,048 autos that year. Eight out of ten car orders requested the much-improved Dynaflow now, and the newest offering was power steering. This was welcome news as all senior-line Buicks weighed in at well over 4,000 pounds.

The division's golden anniversary year was 1953, and sales soared to nearly half a million units. The cars for that year were called all new but bore a strong resemblance to the '52 line. The old reliable straight eight was still in the bottom line "Special," but every other model carried a strong new V-8 under its hood.

The portholes and the gleaming sweepspear
immediately identify this car as a Buick. Wire
wheels by Kelsey-Hayes and the rare chrome
fender skirts are super desirable correct options.

Other series Buicks have the sweepspear, but only
the Roadmaster has the stainless moulding that
extends fully behind the bumper.

In this banner year even convertible production climbed to unreal numbers: 15,500 in all series, with 3,318 of those being the model featured here, the 76-C Roadmaster. This is a big, heavy car, weighing in at 4,250 pounds. It should be remembered in our age of gas-sipping mini-cars, that back in the fifties many American car buyers equated weight with quality. The heavier it was, the better it would "hold the road." If Detroit's knowledge of suspension geometry was in its infancy, the layman's understanding of this factor in handling was nonexistent. The Buick developed its great reputation as a boulevard cruiser in the fifties because their middle-class owners never had occasion to try them out on a curving, hilly road course. I've tried it, and it is more exciting than wise!

Buick always looked more costly than it was. In 1953 the middle line Super series four-door sedan weighed hundreds of pounds more than the DeSoto, yet was cheaper. In size and trim it compared favorably with the '53 Lincoln, yet the Lincoln was nearly $900 more. Small wonder sales zoomed! Four-door Supers alone sold 90,000 units.

Then again, Buick had another card up its sleeve to draw the crowds. For the big anniversary celebration they offered a low production, factory custom convertible called the Skylark. Priced at $5,000, a staggering sum for 1953, it was $1,500 more costly than the top-line Roadmaster ragtop. This remarkable car, alas, handled like every other Buick, but it *looked* like it could win the Indy 500 hands down. It was subtly lower in every dimension: the windshield chopped four inches, the seat cushions nearly on the floor. The doors were cut down and notched in a sweeping curve. As many a bewildered restorer has found out, while it resembles the Roadmaster closely, nearly every panel, fender, door, and deck lid is slightly different. Passenger comfort was not a high priority in designing the Skylark, and the tall driver was left staring right at the top of the windshield

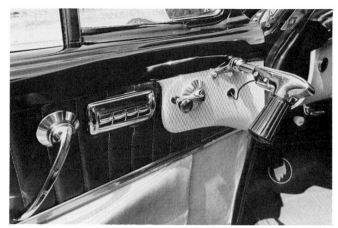

Engine-turned dash, a Buick tradition dating to the thirties, is carried out to the door panel.

Framed headlights are tricky to restore. The black enamel background is usually chipped and shabby. New old-stock parts would be a welcome find for the '53 Buick restorer.

A striking steering wheel and a glittering dash panel mark this as the top-of-the-line series.

Ornate and colorful medallion adorns the lip of the Roadmaster hood.

frame instead of through the glass. Because the seat was abnormally low, the tall driver constantly banged his knee on the steering column. The owner of the production Roadmaster 76-C has a more practical car. Seating is nearly chair high, and vision is better out front and to the rear.

Ken Liska acquired his rare 76-C in 1979 and performed the mechanical restoration himself. A half a million Buicks were made in 1953, but just 4,508 customers ordered this elegant, big convertible. Oddly enough, there seem to be more survivors of the 1,690 Roadmaster Skylarks than the more plentiful 76-C. Ken also applied the Mandarin Red paint but farmed out the upholstery to a professional shop. This owner has endeavored to mount all available options,

First year of the V-8 for Buick, as the faithful valve-in-head straight eight was retired (except in the Buick Special). This is a fully detailed engine room.

A spotlight incorporating a rear-view mirror is a rare and sought after accessory, particularly in new condition.

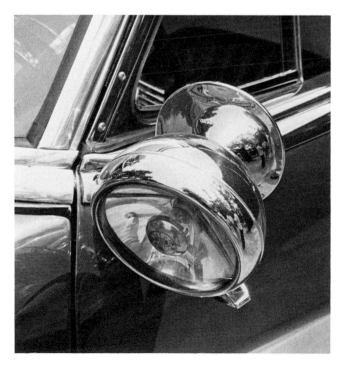

and they include power steering, Buick's Sonomatic radio, factory windshield spotlight with integral rear-view mirror, and even a Buick script deflector on the exhaust pipe. Power seat and top, as well as the incredibly sensitive brakes, were standard on this Roadmaster. Ken's final touch was to mount the Skylark chrome wire wheels, an authentic but seldom-ordered option.

1953 CHRYSLER CROWN IMPERIAL LIMOUSINE

This was the most expensive, heaviest, and longest car Chrysler offered in 1953. It weighed 5,275 pounds and listed at $7,044. Nearly 230 inches long, it rode a wheelbase of 145.5 inches. Needless to say, it was in limited demand and only 111 were built. A similar eight-passenger sedan, lacking the chauffeur division window, was made in 48 copies at about $100 less. Both versions were powered by the big hemi engine, displacing 331 cubic inches and producing 180 horsepower.

Those intrigued by the idea of restoring a limo have a fairly large selection from 1947 through the mid-sixties. The Cadillac retained the classic pre-war look until 1950, when they finally

fashioned a new limo-length body to match their regular models. Chrysler models usually resembled the production New Yorker or Imperial sedan except for added length amidships. Packard had stretched versions of their Clippers on a 148-inch wheelbase after the war, and they did the same to their series made from 1948 through 1950. Production was so low that by the time the 1954 model arrived, limos were only being made to order. Lincoln offered no limos in the fifties but in the sixties provided cars to Lehman-Peterson for conversion to very long and lush limosines that featured bars and color television.

The car featured seems to me the ideal size for a limo. It has a huge rear compartment yet is only seven inches longer than the Cadillac 60-Special sedan offered in 1955 and 1956. It has no waste fins or excessive ornamentation, is large but not ostentatious.

Front view of the Imperial varies only slightly from that of the Chrysler New Yorker. Hood emblem and script set it apart.

There is little wasted overhang in this design. Most of the extra length is usable interior space. It was designed to carry eight passengers.

In profile, the Imperial shows its considerable size. Wheelbase is 145 inches; overall length, 229 inches.

This example was originally the official car of Cardinal Cushing of Boston, Massachusetts. A private collector in New Jersey acquired the car when it was traded, and present owner Bob Porter of Cleveland, Ohio, purchased it from him. Mr. Porter was impressed by the car's sound body and immaculate interior. He elected to drive it back to Ohio, and all went well until the transmission seals, dry from years of storage, let go on the turnpike.

The Powerflite kept performing as long as fluid was present, and that required several quarts being added at every turnpike plaza along the route. Other than the rebuilding of this unit, the Imperial required little restoration. Both the paint and chrome shine like new. Bob finds it the most pleasant of his several cars for long trips—one of which took him to St. Louis, Missouri, and back.

102

Sofa-like rear seat with the arm rest down. The reading lamp was a custom installation for the convenience of former owner, Cardinal Cushing of Boston.

Upholstery in biscuit pattern and wood grain trim are in concours condition, a sign of careful maintenance for thirty years.

Rear doors are the front-opening type and close like the proverbial bank vault on this flawless Imperial limousine.

Chrysler has used many soaring birds on their cars but none more beautiful than this stunning piece from the stylist's studio.

The same winged "V" and red crown found on the hood also adorn the deck lid.

Among candidates to consider for restoration and collecting are the last two models Chrysler made domestically before farming out their limousines to Ghia of Italy. The '55 and '56 models are striking cars, but since only 127 and 169 were made in those respective years, the search will be difficult. The Ghia-built cars of the late fifties are even more flamboyant than the Imperials from which they derived. One should not overlook the Buick offerings, though they go back before the war, from 1937 to 1941. The '41 Limited model is a superb vehicle in every way.

If you want limo luxury, with a private rear compartment closed off from the driver, without outsize length, then the 1953 "owner-driver" Custom Imperial on the regular wheelbase would be the one to hunt down. If "flamboyant" is the way you want to go, find a Ghia-Imperial or a '61 or '62 Cadillac series 75. These models are indeed a car and a half!

Big and heavy (5,275 pounds) as this limo is, the 331 cubic-inch-"hemi" moves it along effortlessly, with nearly the same acceleration as found on the much lighter New Yorker.

Chrysler advertised the Imperial heavily in *Fortune* magazine. Advertising costs per car sold must have been high.

1954 DESOTO FIREDOME SEDAN

This prosaic sedan was selected as an example of a collectible auto that gives a maximum return in practicality. The big, boxy look Chrysler favored won't demand top dollar in this DeSoto version, but oh, what it delivers!

Here is a roomy, spirited auto, full of the amneities we demand today. Thirty years old, it has power steering and brakes, air conditioning, and a fully automatic transmission. It was made in a thrifty six-cylinder version (DeSoto Powermaster), and this V-8 version used the legendary hemi. Even in that 170 horsepower edition, the DeSoto could deliver 20 MPG on the highway. Unbelievably roomy inside, it is just 214 inches long, and that includes a trunk that is cavernous.

The style is big-box Chrysler, short on grace but practical as can be. K. T. Keller, the forceful personality that dictated style and engineering at Chrysler for over a decade, always believed men should not have to remove their hats when riding in his cars. The lofty roof confirms that.

While DeSoto is a so-called orphan car (last model was a 1961), so many parts interchange with the Chrysler line that repair is not a real problem. The last year for the boxy look was 1954, and DeSotos would grow longer, sleeker, heavier, and more bechromed with Chrysler in the years ahead.

If you want a package for day in, day out driving, it is hard to surpass the 1954 DeSoto line. You might prefer the almost sporty two-door hardtop, or a four-door station wagon. Along with the luxury Imperials of the sixties, these cars

The toothy grille of the DeSoto was a surprisingly expensive design to build, as anyone who has disassembled one can attest. The "floating" effect was quite stylish in 1954.

Sharing the same body as many other Chrysler products, DeSoto had a loyal following. The '54 line were fine cars and great values.

DeSoto was "built to last" and was handicapped only by a lack of styling distinction in the marketplace. This sedan had room, comfort, and sound engineering to recommend it, today as in 1954.

are cheap. DeSoto sedans and wagons are rarely priced over $1,000 in unrestored condition, and I have been offered decent ones in the $300-to-$500 range.

Chrysler has made over two million DeSotos since the marque was created in 1928. They were built to high standards with the best materials and were, as their ads stated, "Built to Last."

Cal and Lori Middleton have owned this DeSoto since 1973. They found it in pristine, pampered condition and have preserved it that way ever since. In that time they have added just 4,000 summertime miles to the original 36,000 on the odometer. It has always been a local car, purchased new from Parker Motors, on the old Ohio canal waterway at Canal Fulton, Ohio.

Dash layout of the DeSoto was modern and uncluttered. This was the first year a DeSoto could be had with a fully automatic transmission.

With all that room inside, Chrysler engineers still provided extremely deep doors, a bonus in the event of a side impact collision.

Other DeSotos have a higher degree of collectability, notably in the 1956 Adventurer. They would use this name again on later models, but the 1956 is the one to have. This production car had a high-performance version of the hemi that put out 320 horsepower. One car actually ran in the Daytona Speed Weeks. Only 996 were made, and just two color combinations were offered, though some were repainted later. Gold and white, and gold and black were the buyer's

Roomy is an understatement when describing the four-door sedan. Cavernous would be more appropriate. Note the assist bars on the back of the front seat.

Fake air scoop adorns the hood of the big Firedome DeSoto.

choice. This is probably the most sought after DeSoto, along with the '56 Indy 500 Pace car model. These two are high-dollar cars, ranging up to $7,000 to $10,000 in mint condition.

It is hard to believe, looking at the Middletons' DeSoto gleaming in the sun, that the paint, chrome, and mint-appearing interior are thirty years old. Perhaps in this case, one can be excused for falling back on that old cliché, "They don't build 'em like they used to."

1954 MERCURY MONTEREY TWO-DOOR HARDTOP

Postwar Mercury development into the late fifties went through four stages: The '46, '47, and '48 series were warmed-over prewar styles, almost indistinguishable from Fords. In 1949 a new "Merc" appeared. Totally unlike the new Ford, it shared its body shell instead with the bottom line Lincoln. Good news for Mercury, not so good for staid Lincoln customers, who expected a certain amount of unique style for their larger dollar outlay. Sales were great through 1951, and the round, slippery Merc shape would become familiar in customizing shops across the country over the next decade.

It came as something of a surprise then, to see Ford revert in 1952 to the re-trimmed Ford look on the new Mercury line. Compare a '52 Ford Crestline Victoria hardtop with that year's

In contrast to the Olds hardtops, the Merc is light and lively looking. The bold spear running the length of the car adds to that image.

new Mercury Custom hardtop. Only the grille is substantially different. Of course all Mercs were V-8 powered, while many Fords were sixes. Ford kept tinkering with their overhead valve V-8, promised for the '52 line, but it was delayed until the 1954 models. The trusty flathead V-8 that was retained in the 1952 through 1953 cars was popular then and is so today.

The '52 body was well proportioned and would serve until 1956. One of the real innovations, taken for granted today, is the combined bumper and grille—considered fairly radical then. Finally, in 1954 the OHV V-8 that had already been offered in Lincolns became the basic powerplant in the Mercury line. Both the Custom and the upper level Monterey shared the cast-iron V-8 of 256 cubes that turned out 162 horsepower. A major mechanical improvement in the '54 model was the switch to ball-joint front suspension that greatly improved handling. Buyers could choose from standard three-speed manual shifting, with or without overdrive, or Merc-O-

The new Mercury for 1954 followed the trend to combine bumper and grille—and did so very effectively. The huge simulated air scoop on the hood repeats the grille design.

Rear view of the Monterey is classically simple and uncluttered. Shallow deck lid, however, meant a high lift when putting suitcases in the trunk.

Matic drive. This last option would start in intermediate, then quickly shift to high, giving fairly sluggish acceleration.

Mercury covered the price range from $2,194 to $2,800, with the big wagon at the top end. The super collectible of 1954, other than the 76-B, the Monterey convertible, is the aptly named Sun Valley. Similar to the Crestline Skyliner offered by Ford, the Sun Valley split the roof of a two-door hardtop and inserted a sheet of green tinted aircraft-type plexiglass in the front half, over the front seat. Some owners will tell you it was not only great for letting the sun in, but also good for baking potatoes on the dash. At $2,582, the car was popular enough to draw almost ten-thousand orders. John James, the New Philadelphia, Ohio, owner of the 1954 Monterey shown here has a frayed Sun Valley tucked away in the recesses of his roomy garage, marked for future restoration.

His Siren Red Monterey hardtop is a classic restoration story of how luck, knowledge, and ingenuity can substitute for big dollars in completing a fine car project. John had been an admirer of the 1952 Merc since his navy days in the mid fifties. In 1961 he bought a '54 hardtop and drove it for years, finally scrapping it out. The red and black interior was so flawless, he carefully removed and stored it. In 1969 he noted a parts car Monterey at a local gas station. The front fenders were missing as was the complete drivetrain. The body shell was so solid he located the owner to discuss a possible purchase. The owner happily offered to drop it off in Mr. James's driveway for the grand and total sum of fifteen dollars.

John then recalled a four-door Mercury he had seen in a local wrecking yard. A hurried visit proved it was the same year, with just 40,000 miles on the odometer. He was offered the overdrive unit for $30, or the entire car for $100. This find produced not only a perfect drivetrain (only a valve grind was required) but a perfect deck lid and various other parts.

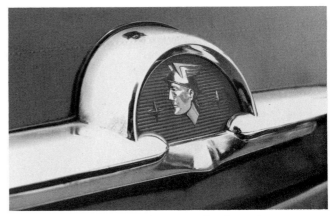

Medallion on trunk lid is a work of art depicting the car's namesake: the winged messenger, Mercury.

Bold slashes of chrome mark the sharply angled rear fender outline.

An immaculate interior that was salvaged from a high-mileage Merc being scrapped out for parts.

Designers made a conscious effort to simulate the look of an airplane cockpit on the Merc dash. It took an ingenious use of cables, but they achieved the desired illusion.

Triple-ridge design on taillight lens is repeated on rear fender in chrome moldings.

Remembering a California car he had bought taillight units from, John stopped by on a family trip to the West Coast and inspected the car. Perfect front fenders were pulled for $60. Before he was through, parts from a half-dozen cars found their way on to John's new hardtop. Many trim pieces are N.O.S., and only the bumpers required replating. This conscientious restorer removed side and rear glass from a parts car to make a perfect match of glass. The $15 body had nontinted glass, and John wanted the tinted option. In the dozen years since completing his

This correct, low mileage 256-cubic-inch V-8 now residing in the nicely detailed engine compartment of this Monterey came from a $100 parts car.

restoration, the James family has put about 10,000 miles on their scarlet beauty. Interestingly enough, the still immaculate red-and-black interior has well over 100,000 miles on it!

What are the choice Mercurys of the postwar era? It is a wide range from the 1946 model to such low-production series as the '69 and '70 Marauder X-100 hardtops. This was a super-loaded, super-powered Thunderbird market offering, with only some 7,500 produced over the two-year run.

The prime choices would have to include the scarce Sportsman convertible of 1946 and 1947, priced in *Old Car Guide* at $30,000 in mint condition. The '47 and '48 wagons look prewar in their woody elegance and are equally scarce,

but considerably less expensive. The hardtop style shown in this profile can be had in the early flathead V-8 style ('52 or '53) or this OHV version. The 1956 Montclair hardtop or convertible are attractive cars and have not as yet attracted the rabid following of the '49 through '51 Mercs. Later examples would have to include the Cougar, an upscale clone of the Mustang. Cougar convertibles are a sleeper at present, including models up to 1972, when the ragtop saw a run of just 1,240 cars. This writer saw one of those scarce ones offered in decent restorable condition recently at $1,800.

Whatever direction you go, Mercurys seem a safe bet both for pleasure and for future dollar appreciation.

1955 CHEVROLET BEL AIR TWO-DOOR NOMAD WAGON

I f the Corvette has earned its place as the American sportscar of the postwar era, then the quintessential station wagon of this period has to be the Chevy Nomad. Few people realize, however, that the Nomad developed directly from the original 1953 Corvette.

Harley Earl, vice-president of styling for GM, designed the first open "Vette" as a show car. The reception was so warm, Earl thought about doing variations of the design theme, even as Chevrolet was putting the car into limited production. Three of those spinoffs were hand built: a fastback ironically named Corvair, a hardtop 'Vette just like the convertible, and a striking station wagon. They coined the name Nomad for it, but a wagon this low, sleek, and sporty couldn't be called a station wagon, so Nomad "sport wagon" it became.

This striking profile is like no other Chevy and no other wagon. The curving roof pillar and sharply raked rear hatch are unique to the Nomad.

In January of 1954, these gems were put before the public at the Waldorf-Astoria Motorama in New York City. The Nomad was a smash hit, and a major effort was launched to include a version of its style in the 1955 Chevrolet line, already far advanced. The wagon that resulted from this crash program was a beauty, but it was more inspired by, than derived from, the sleek Waldorf Nomad. The key features that survived the transfer were the fluted roof design, the swooping roof pillar, and the unique glass treatment. What did not survive was the round 'Vette nose, low silhouette, and bobbed rear-end body line. The windshield rake was more vertical than that of the Waldorf version, and the front end of the car matched the rest of the '55 line of Chevys. Nevertheless, the public liked what they saw, and over six thousand were ordered.

Among postwar collected cars, the 1955–57 Chevrolets are high on everyone's list. As happens on rare occasions, a number of fine engineering achievements coincided with out-

standing styling to produce a line of exceptional automobiles. A new V-8, first in a Chevy in thirty-six years, was the centerpiece. Around it was arrayed a new ball-joint front suspension, a new steering linkage, a modern 12-volt electrical system, and, better late than never, Studebaker's favorite option: overdrive. Over the next twenty years America's teenagers would grow up with, tinker, repair, and hot rod with that 265 cubic inch V-8 engine.

Good engineering was profitable, too. To one accustomed to traditional Packard, Cadillac-type construction, it would be disconcerting to see your new Chevy on the lube rack and not find a big 'X' member under the body. The box section that carried the front suspension and one light channel member at the rear were all that were needed for stiffness. The fully boxed side rails did the job with a weight savings of nearly 20 percent and some savings in manufacturing cost.

The true Nomad has a brief life span—just three versions through the 1957 model year. The '56 had enough changes in looks to further dilute its appeal. More mundane than sporty, the distinctive egg-crate grille was gone, and the pure line of the profile now had a Buick-like spear of two-tone color treatment. The '57 was more like a sedan than a sportscar. Both the '56 and '57 gave up the full-wheel fender cutout, which had been one of the most distinctive styling elements of the near-classic first Nomad. But none of these changes can be blamed for the modest sales. The simple fact was that a really useful wagon needed four doors, and the Nomad was a six-passenger two door.

Headlight crowns and the full-width bumper guard are prized accessories and dress up this flawless Nomad considerably.

Sharp slope of the Nomad rear end is evident from this angle. Bumper ends are sought after accessories. Roof rack is a practical addition the owner added but is not authentic.

From the front, the Nomad resembles all other 1955 Chevrolets. Many collectors feel the 1955 "eggcrate" grille is the best of the fifties Chevy production.

Ribbed molding on the rear hatch are a Nomad trademark. Not visible is a ribbed design in the roof as well.

Spotless room where the five main-bearing Bel Air V-8 lives in this Nomad wagon.

Beautiful interior done in the original wafflecloth material. Lack of four doors was the one great deficiency in the attractive Nomad, and it hurt sales.

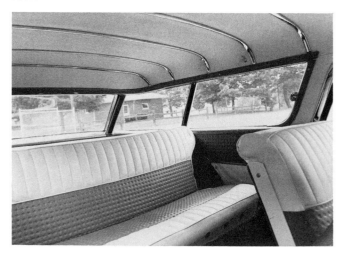

Low production of collectible cars is a two-edged sword. It makes them valuable but, at the same time, hard to find.

Old Cars Price Guide puts the 1955 Nomad in a range from $15,000 in No. 1 restored condition to a low of $2,200 in No. 5 condition (a car almost complete and needing total restoration). The 1956 model lists at only a few hundred under that range although it is definitely less sought out than the '55.

The car shown here is owned by Joyce Talcott of Akron, Ohio. It was a total restoration by an Ohio firm that specializes in fifties Chevrolets, Hamilton Auto Restoration.

It should be mentioned that Chevrolet owners of 1955–57 models have the same huge army of reproduction parts suppliers as do owners of classic Mustang models, and this can greatly accelerate a car project.

What can you expect to find in your Nomad search? Among the several dozen offered recently

Just so you don't forget what car you're driving, Chevrolet has thoughtfully provided a motif of their logo on the panel beneath the padded dash of this Nomad wagon.

in the pages of the three leading hobby periodicals I found these: A '57 beautiful original, always maintained, at $8,500. A '55 show car marred with numerous "improvements" (the wrong wheels, add-on air, radials, stereo tape deck, etc.), asking price is $10,500. A '57 Nomad with original factory air in need of restoration, at $2,500. Another 1956 with all original equipment, even decent paint, a rust-free Wyoming car, offered at $2,800. With such a variety of offerings, caution is indicated. Don't lose sight of the value of an original, carefully maintained car. Many times the cost of undoing inappropriate "improvements" is as great as or even greater than that of a correct restoration.

You might have some luck in the real world of your local paper's classifieds. There is an ad in my paper today: "1956 Nomad, original car with spare parts, $2,300."

Might just give him a ring. . . .

Skid bars line the floor of the Nomad. The slanted hatch has a tendency to leak in a heavy rain.

1956 STUDEBAKER POWER HAWK

Studebaker, which eventually closed their South Bend, Indiana, plant in 1964, had begun as a carriage works in 1852. The company's history came to my attention in 1958 when I purchased a used '52 Landcruiser and the key fob advised me I owned a Century Anniversary Studebaker. I've owned seven Studes since then, and all have been notable for two characteristics: unique styling and durability.

In the postwar period, Studebaker may be said to have had three great moments in the sun. This is a serious claim, considering they rarely ranked better in the market than tenth place. First,

Studebaker got the jump on the whole mighty Detroit industry by launching a really new car in 1947. The critics carped, "Is it going or is it coming?" But this bold and innovative model established the parameters of auto design for a decade.

Studebaker's second great moment was the production of the Loewy sport coupe of 1953 (more properly, Raymond Loewy–Bob Bourke Starlight coupe and Starliner hardtop). This was that rare occasion when the directors allowed a "dream-car" concept to go directly into production. The resulting car has appeared on virtually every expert's "ten best" list of all time.

Their third triumph was, of course, the 1963 Avanti—possibly the purest automotive shape ever placed over wheels, in a style class with the coffin-nose Cord of 1936 and the 1938 Lincoln Zephyr.

Why then, isn't there a gleaming Studebaker

This first year of the Hawk was derived from the famed Bourke-Loewy coupe of 1953. A bold new hood, grille, and rear deck made it quite another car.

The new deck lid not only changed the car's lines but also added needed trunk space.

Considered one of the most beautiful profiles in motoring, the Studebaker coupes, hardtops, and Hawks are far more affordable than the early Mustangs.

showroom on Main Street in your town today? No company capable of such excellence seems to have had the misfortunes of Studebaker. They reveled in the success of the 1947 model through 1952 but never applied the profits to updating plant technology. Studebaker kept its packed-earth floors decades after this twenties' practice had given way to poured concrete. When the low and sleek Loewy-Bourke two-door models took the country by storm, management decreed that 80 percent of production should be sedans, because that had always been their mix. The sedans filled storage yards, while back orders accumulated for the rakish hardtops.

The 1953 models were really the last "clean sheet of paper" cars from the company until its tortured demise in a Canadian plant in 1965. Incredibly, the last twelve years would see one great facelift after another from the basic 1953 platform.

An exception to the series of superficial face-lifts was the body concept of the Avanti, but even it sat on an older convertible frame. Appearing in 1963, the Avanti was the new car that would save Studebaker, so they hoped. More than a pretty face, it set twenty-nine production auto speed records at Bonneville Salt Flats in Utah. Orders poured in for the less-than-$4,500 beauty. Just as it appeared that the company finally had a money maker, a new complication arose. The company making those beautiful fiberglass bodies became "unavailable" to Studebaker, which was forced to enter this alien technology under great pressure and build their own bodies.

But back in 1956 they needed to perform yet another low-budget facelift on the aging Loewy coupes and hardtops. Although prior to 1955, facelifts had been mostly confined to trim and new dashes, now sheet-metal changes would be essential to give the two-door a new look. Fortunately, the same team, headed by Raymond Loewy and Robert Bourke, that had created the original 1953 line was available for this effort.

Classic purity of line, complete with the rare stainless steel wire wheel covers.

Swivel-out windows were featured on the coupes, hardtop side windows cranked down into the body. Chrome side trim visible here is from the Sky Hawk series, not normally listed for the coupe-bodied Hawks.

Black-and-silver (polished aluminum) wheel and dash are sporty looking. Radio is out being repaired, and an original clock is being sought to complete this driver-level restoration.

Studebaker crest is found on both grille and deck lid latch.

The resulting Hawk line (and few cars had a name that fit so well) seemed bolder, more powerful, and really new. Yet, if one removes the new hood and deck lid and replaces them with those from a '53 Starliner, one is amazed at how clever those changes were. By sharply raising the lines of the hood and deck lid almost to the horizontal and squaring off the front and rear of the body shell, they brought out a different car at minimal production costs.

The crowning stroke from a marketing view was creation of a powerhouse performer in the top-of-the-line model, the Golden Hawk. This was accomplished by shoehorning-in Packard's Clipper Custom V-8 of 352 cubic inches. With an output of 275 horsepower it was the most powerful Stude ever. This marriage came about because Packard had merged with the Studebaker Corporation in 1954, a partnership that would last four short years. This top model carried the twin-ultramatic, a trouble-plagued unit built by Packard at great cost. I owned one in the sixties that had a disconcerting habit of jumping into reverse at traffic lights.

The Hawk line consisted of four models. The top two were the hardtops, the Golden Hawk and the Skyhawk. The coupe version came in a smaller V-8, the Power Hawk, and a six, the Flight Hawk. As far as exterior styling was concerned, all shared the same front end. Side trim varied on each model, and only the Golden Hawk had vestigial fins, which were made of fiberglass.

The Power Hawk illustrated here enjoyed a production run of 7,095 units. All Hawk models made totaled 19,165. For Studebaker, this was a significant segment of their nearly 70,000 cars sold in the 1956 model year (down sharply from the 116,333 cars sold in 1955).

It is interesting to note that these four new Hawks outsold the one model Thunderbird of 1956 (16,000 to 15,000). The Golden Hawk was actually ten dollars higher than the T'bird. A restored Golden Hawk today, however, may command only one-third to one-quarter of the price of the classic T'bird. Why Studebaker never revived the last 1952 commander convertible in Hawk sheet metal is one of the great mysteries of South Bend thinking.

Studebaker purists who have studied the Power Hawk photos presented here are undoubtedly confused: How can that be a Power Hawk when the side trim is from the Skyhawk series? I recovered this coupe in 1981 from a Virginia shed where it had waited patiently for some nineteen years. As the restoration proceeded through various stages, I recalled a conversation I had had with a Studebaker dealer on Long Island, New York, in 1963. He mentioned that buyers would occasionally want a color scheme on one model that did not provide a suitable separation line. In the case of the Power Hawk, the car was offered in solid colors only, with the sole option of a contrasting roof. According to this dealer, he had ordered the Skyhawk trim as an option on new Hawk coupes, and the factory had obliged, at additional cost.

Realizing I would be explaining this contradiction at every Studebaker car meet for the rest of my life, I nevertheless located a set of N.O.S. Skyhawk trim and converted the partial two-tone paint to full, Skyhawk style, two tone. I believe it makes the car appear lower and longer, and is worth the minor controversy over authenticity.

Other Studebakers to consider would have to include any of the convertibles from 1947 through 1952. The first hardtop offered in 1952 is still striking in its clean lines. The exotic Speedster is probably the most sought after of the 1955 series, marred only by awful color schemes. The Conestoga wagons of 1954 and 1955 and the later Lark converts round out a considerable selection.

Unrestored Studebakers seem to share with Imperials the distinction of being the most undervalued of all postwar makes—which means there are some fine buys out there.

This original Sweepstakes V-8, a cast-iron 259-cubic-inch, ran well out of nineteen years dead storage. The compartment has yet to be detailed.

These hard-to-find lenses were of fragile plastic, but reproductions are available today.

1956 PACKARD FOUR HUNDRED HARDTOP COUPE

A number of great old names closed up shop in the fierce competition of the late fifties, but none caused the traumatic shock of the passing of Packard. It is safe to say that no American car builder had made as many great automobiles over as long a period of time as had Packard, and that includes Cadillac. Where they failed, it appears from the comfortable hindsight of twenty-five years, was in not recognizing the changed criteria people were using to select their cars. Packard had built their whole image, from the twin-six of the teens through the Super eights of the thirties, on

"The Four Hundred" represented Packard's last effort at a full-sized luxury hardtop. Despite improvements over the prototype 1955 model, only 3,224 were sold.

engineering quality. They bet not on bold innovation, but on solid engineering and superb materials, mated to classically stylish body design.

In the fifties the stylist emerged supreme, and a car's looks alone pulled customers from one make to another. All cars were presumed to be good mechanically. This necessitated yearly facelifts that were noticeably different, and Packard had never believed in yearly change for cosmetic effect alone.

Before the closing of the huge plant in Detroit, in 1956; the retreat to South Bend; and the ill-starred marriage to a failing Studebaker, Packard had just three major designs in the postwar era.

Through 1947, the company relied on the original Clipper series, introduced in 1941. This was a graceful and stylish bridge from the boxy

From every angle, styling was clean and crisp. Three color combinations were offered along with full power, including such touches as dual-power antennas.

A very big car must depend on scale and proportion to look attractive. Here, horizontal ribbing below the trunk repeated in the taillight frame seemingly reduces the sheer size of this Packard to some degree.

series of the thirties into the new unified look. More could have been done with it.

This was followed by the 1948–1950 model. Often criticized for its bulging lines, these cars were mechanically outstanding and built to high standards.

In 1951 came the basic new design that was as up-to-date as any other Detroit product. It would be facelifted into 1956 as the last full-sized true Packards made by the company at the East Grand Boulevard factory in Detroit.

In that last year of the big car, Packard offered the Packard Executive line and the Clipper line, as a lower-priced series, plus the elite Caribbean sub series, consisting of a two-door hardtop and a stunning convertible. These were in addition to the basic Packard Patrician sedan.

These were, finally, very advanced machines, beautifully styled, with the leading engineering innovations of the day. The big new V-8 produced from 240 horsepower in the DeLuxe Clipper, to 310 in the 374-cubic-inch version the Caribbean employed.

Torsion-level suspension, an engineering marvel that kept the car level and softly sprung no matter the load or the road, finally had the bugs worked out. Early problems with hydraulic lifters in the new V-8 were a thing of the past. The Packard stylists had designed a first in that the seats in the Caribbean were reversible, brocade on one side, leather on the other. The improved Ultramatic now worked from a battery of push buttons.

All to no avail—the public was not moved. Calendar year sales in 1956 were a paltry 13,432 units, down from the marginal figure of 70,000 vehicles in the previous year when this last-gasp styling had been introduced.

So began the move to South Bend and oblivion in 1958. The less said about the strange trim tacked on the Stude President wearing Packard wheel covers, the better. They thought to keep something, anything, in the showrooms of the Packard dealers, along with the hybrid Packard

A very mint and original interior are displayed in this exceptional "Four Hundred."

Packard crest is on the brushed-metal piller of the big hardtop. The plastic tube inside is for the air-conditioning system.

Packard also included "Dagmars" in their bumper design, but this is an outstanding grille, assembled by the owner from all-new old-stock parts.

Torsion-level suspension was emphasized in Packard ads, but the public had heard of the teething troubles the system had in 1955 models. The 1956 models were quite trouble free, to no avail.

Hawk, until a new, true Packard would rise from the ashes. When it was first displayed in New York, I made a special trip to examine the Packard Predicter, the car that would save the company. In retrospect, it had an Edsel-like appearance and reflected styling gone wild rather than the purity of line that once symbolized the Packard Motor Car. It is just as well it never saw production.

The "400" illustrated here was purchased by William Majors of Richfield Ohio, in 1973. It had sustained front end damage in a collision but was a low mileage original, having run just 41,000 miles.

Mr. Majors replaced both front fenders and grille with N.O.S. parts he located. The original bumpers were replated, but the fine interior is original. The ultramatic transmission needed to be rebuilt, and that was accomplished with only a new oil pump for the smooth-running engine. The torsion-level suspension system is in good working order and still surprises passengers with the quality of the ride. Only 3,224 Four Hundred hardtops were made in 1956. It represents an outstanding value today, costing much less than the sought after Caribbean convertibles.

Other favorites of mine include the eight-cylinder Clippers of 1946–47, the custom eight convertible of 1948–50 and the last straight eight top-of-the-line convertible, the Caribbean of 1954. Possibly the best value in a top-flight Packard using this fabulous nine main-bearing engine would be the Patrician sedan of 1953–54, which in unrestored condition can be found for as little as one thousand dollars. "Ask the Man Who Owns One," and that will seem a bargain, indeed.

This dash seems rather busy, perhaps because everything is chromed. The Ultramatic pushbutton shift is in the foreground.

The so-called cathedral taillight units. Sheltering lights under an overhang of sheet metal was a fixation with auto stylists in the fifties. This Packard has the "frenched" lights both fore and aft.

1960 RAMBLER AMERICAN DELUXE SEDAN

Despite America's eternal love for the big car, there has always been someone, somewhere, thoroughly convinced the right kind of small car will take the market by storm. Young people today will agree, asserting that it took the Datsun and Honda Civic to do just that. Middle-aged folks will disagree, stoutly insisting the Volkswagon Beetle woke up America with its fifteen million unit sales. The fact is that the Beetle, the Ford Falcon, the Hudson Jet, the Aero Willys, and the Henry J. would never have braved the market-

Some collectors scorn bottom-line models of basic transportation cars. A new trend sees hobbyists seeking out examples such as this 1960 Rambler American sedan.

place if the Nash Rambler hadn't blazed the trail so successfully.

After one of the longest and most complex development periods for any new car, the Rambler was introduced as a unitized body convertible in 1950. From the mid-thirties to 1948, George Mason, president of Nash, pressed experiments with engines of 2, 3, and 4 cylinders, and vehicles of 2, 3, and 4 wheels. He wisely settled for a fine six-cylinder engine already in production and offered a most unusual convertible; its doors were full height and closed on roof rails that doubled as railroad tracks for the fabric top, drawn up by steel cables. It looked a little strange with its top down, but the public loved it. That was quickly followed by a two-door wagon and a perky hardtop in 1951. With names like Country Club and Greenbrier, Mason

Dash is almost military in its austere look. Everything the driver need know is in that one dial on the American's metal dash.

The perky engine is larger than the battery in this Rambler. The 90 horsepower L-head six delivered more than adequate power in the small car.

Even in the four-door version of the compact American, rear-seat passengers rode ahead of the axle.

Solid workmanship without frills was the Rambler watchword. All the doors on this sedan open and close faultlessly after twenty-three years of use.

was not yet aiming at the bottom-dollar transportation market, but at the second-car market—people who already had a Buick or Cadillac in the garage.

The convertible Landau model started a trend, convincing the doubting public that a car on a 100-inch wheelbase, just 176 inches long overall, could still accommodate five people in comfort. Nash shrewdly sold the Rambler loaded with no-cost options—such as radio, foam cushions, electric clock, and turn signals—at a reasonable $1,810.

Rambler sales climbed and in the three-year span from 1959 through 1961 helped put the reborn American Motors firm into fourth place in sales. New President George Romney insisted a four-door sedan version was possible, something company engineers had stoutly fought since 1949, and the car featured here was the result.

Still capable of delivering both peppy performance and 25–30 MPG on the highway, this compact sedan is owned by Ken Vanderbush of Akron, Ohio. Though it has wintered five years in the midwest rust belt, the car is in excellent condition, mostly due to an early Zeibart treatment and the fact that its earlier life was spent in sunny Florida. Ken still needs an original air cleaner for the 196-cubic-inch engine and plans to mount the correct wide white 600-by-15 inch tires on his American. The engine was recently overhauled and now has 109,000 miles on it.

While automatic was available, this bottom-of-the-line example has a standard shift. It is one of 22,593 produced in 1960, weighs 2,474 pounds, and listed for just $1,844 when new.

Detroit may have finally turned the corner in their deadly battle of the imports, but they can't say they weren't shown the way. George Mason, Meade Moore, George Romney, and an inspired group of engineers and workers at Nash blazed a trail in those early postwar years that was perhaps forgotten too quickly.

Generic streamlining might be the way to characterize the American's smooth lines.

*Trim and neat, Americans led the way to
American Motors' first billion-dollar year—1960
when nearly half a million cars left AM plants.*

1961 LINCOLN CONTINENTAL SEDAN

America's postwar family of luxury cars consisted of Cadillac, Lincoln, Packard, and Imperial. A few other makes had models that contested in the market, such as the Buick Roadmaster and the Olds 98, but for flat-out luxury, these four were the top contenders.

Surprisingly, Packard was still outselling Cadillac in 1950, though many of their sales were of bottom-line, plain-Jane models. Still, Cadillac, with 103,857 cars produced in that model year, trailed Packard by 3,000 vehicles. Lincoln sold 32,574 cars, and Chryslers' Imperial just topped the 10,000 figure in 1950.

A decade later saw the introduction of a new

The most serious postwar competition Cadillac ever had, the 1961 Lincoln was a major effort by Ford to contend for the luxury car market.

luxury Lincoln that many consider among the landmark automotive designs of the postwar era. What makes this car remarkable is how totally it broke with the five Lincolns preceding it. The taut, crisply styled car of 1953–55 had by 1957 given way to a huge barge of a highway cruiser—too long, too gaudily decorated, too willowy in construction for anything but the smoothest of uncrowded highways. A few figures demonstrate this move to excess: The 1953 Lincoln's wheelbase was 123 inches; its overall length, 214 inches; weight 4,150 pounds. The comparable 1960 model had grown by half a ton more in weight; the wheelbase, to 131 inches; and the ornate body was over a foot longer.

The striking new '61 model, while weighing in just under 5,000 pounds, was actually shorter than the 1953 Capri by an inch and rode on the same-length 123-inch wheelbase. It is deceptive

The first year, 1961, Lincoln is considered the one to have, as the car grew in weight into 1967. The curved side glass was changed to flat in 1964.

The rear deck lid nested between knife-edge moldings that ran from front fenders to rear tail lamps.

While the body was straight edged and slab sided, there were plenty of graceful curves both front and rear on the impressive new Lincoln.

of design—this elegant auto of Elwood Engel—in that it seems to get smaller every day you drive it, despite its big-car appearance.

A really bold and daring concept had been developing in Ford's boardroom over several years. A brand-new plant at Wixom, Michigan, was built solely for Thunderbird and Lincoln production. Their unitized construction allowed both cars to be intermixed on the assembly line. The cream of Ford's people, engineers and blue-collar alike, were indoctrinated in the cause of quality goals never before attempted with a standard-production automobile. Every Lincoln underwent a series of tests that put Detroit's routine "ten minutes, then out the door check" to shame.

Every engine in every car was run on a stand for three hours. Selected transmissions were run on dynamometers at 95 MPH for an hour. The exhaustively tested completed car was then turned over to a test driver. A twelve-mile road course was then run with 189 check points involving every aspect of the car's chassis and drive train. Even the specifications for the window lift motors were aimed at providing a twenty-year life.

So-called suicide doors puzzled some shoppers. Front-opening rear doors, however, make entry and exit easier on the Lincoln.

Heavy doors had genuine wood veneer inserts above the padded armrests.

Ford further simplified their production problems by fielding just two models, both simply designated Lincoln Continental. One was the four-door sedan here featured, the other a nearly identical four-door convertible. The sedan was priced at $6,067, and the convertible at $6,713. The cars were fully equipped, and the option list was a short one. Air conditioning added $504, tinted glass $53, and a six-way power seat and cruise control were the remaining choices. Power door locks, handsome walnut appliqué, and a rear-seat radio speaker were standard equipment on both models.

This timeless design was recognized by a bronze medal from the prestigious Industrial Design Institute. *Car Life* magazine featured it as a breakthrough machine and yet, disappointing to Ford, sales of these two new models barely exceeded the dozen assorted versions of the 1960 land yacht it replaced. If it is true that "cream rises to the top," then one must come to the conclusion that many buyers did not know cream when they saw it.

Ford hoped for sales in the 50,000 to 75,000 unit range. Over the life of the Engel-designed Lincoln, from 1961 to 1967, the convertible found just 3,000 buyers annually, while sedan sales rose from an initial 22,303 only to the 35,000 unit range. Cadillac outsold Lincoln approximately four to one during this period.

From a collector's viewpoint, the first three years have the edge in that the curved glass, shorter body, and original design holds up best aesthetically. Every one of the seven-year run of four-door convertibles is, of course, highly collectible. Some hobbyists are put off by horror tales of the highly complex disappearing top that Ford employed on this model. Its one glaring fault is that it nearly fills the trunk space when in the stowed position. I can testify, however, to having run a '61 convertible daily for three years, summer and winter, without a single top malfunction, and this was in a car with 137,000 miles on the odometer. It should also be mentioned that the '61 came with a two-barrel carburetor. On a 1,500-mile trip carrying four people, that well-used Lincoln delivered exactly 20 MPG.

Considering all the outstanding postwar models produced in America and abroad, the '61 Lincoln takes a back seat to none in sheer quality of engineering, materials, handling, and comfort, plus that indefinable appearance element we call "class." For the collector of the mid-eighties, it represents one of the very best values for the money, whether it ever surges ahead in resale value or not. It has been esti-

This Lincoln symbol rode the otherwise-unadorned hood of the bold new Continental. Buyers were given a marble paperweight with this same ornament as a promotion gift by Lincoln dealers.

Detail of the rear corner. Beauty of concept and execution won the '61 Lincoln a bronze medal from the prestigious Industrial Design Institute.

A huge dash matched the angular lines of the body itself. Wood appliqués were of walnut.

Collectible Lincolns are still plentiful. This 1964 model was offered at $1,800 by a used-car dealer recently. A rusted out rear bumper seemed the only obvious flaw.

mated that to build a four-door luxury car in America to this standard today would require a sticker price in excess of $40,000.

The car shown here was a fortunate find for owner John Glassner of Akron, Ohio. Mr. Glassner operates a truck repair business and is familiar with old cars native to his area, often referred to as the rust belt due to the heavy use of salt for snow removal.

His Lincoln, however, was in the constant care of a chauffeur-driver from new. Its lady owner preferred riding in the front passenger seat and, as the ads sometimes claim, this Lincoln's back seat has literally never been used. The ash trays are immaculate as well. Mileage is in the forty-thousand range, and Mr. Glassner operates the car only in fair weather. Salt never had a chance at this Lincoln as it was stored during the winter season.

All '61 Lincolns had automatic drive mated to this 300-horsepower, 430-cubic-inch V-8. It was capable of delivering 20 MPG on the highway with four passengers aboard. Rear-opening hood was an unusual feature.

Just one small item required plating and proved a puzzling, if minor, mystery. The key cover plate on the front passenger door was badly worn. There was a simple explanation: The chauffeur would routinely unlock the passenger door with his key and help his employer into the car. While he walked around to the driver's side, she would reach over and unlock his door!

Other Lincolns to consider from the postwar era might include the sleek four-door fastback Cosmopolitan Sport sedan of 1949, the '54 or '55 Capri two-door hardtop, or the '56 Premiere two-door hardtop. The low-production Mark II of 1956 and 1957 is a near classic and, at far fewer dollars, so is the Mark III of 1969–71.

Lincoln brochures dwelt on the superb materials and workmanship in every Lincoln. The writer has seen 200,000-mile examples with not a thread broken in the interior.

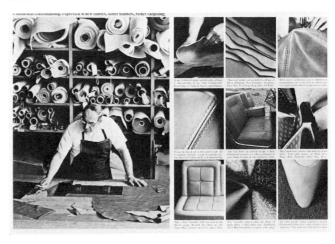

1963 PONTIAC GRAND PRIX HARDTOP

We all know how the ill-fated Edsel came into being: Ford saw a marketing gap between their regular line and the higher-priced Mercury models. The Edsel was meant to fill that slot and keep the original Ford customer in the family. Though the Edsel failed abjectly, the theory was sound.

As far back as 1921, General Motors conceived the "moving up" approach to selling cars. They needed a new make to fit between the popular Chevrolet and their more expensive Oakland. So was born the Pontiac, an immediate success from its debut in 1926.

The restyled Grand Prix for 1963 had a very clean body shell. Even the identifying badges were small and discreet.

So successful was it that it killed off all demand for the Oakland in a few short years. For decades the Pontiac was the car you moved up to from your Chevy. More power, more lush trim concealed the huge number of parts that remained pure Chevrolet. It was a great formula, because there was little need for innovation in both cars, only the Chevy. This so-called commonality concept helped build GM into the giant it is today, as it accomplished both marketplace saturation and major production economies.

Pontiac stayed prosperous until the early fifties, when the marketplace changed. At that time there developed different market perceptions of cars for the young and sporty, and cars for the older and more sedate.

The legendary "Bunkie" Knudsen took over as division manager in 1956 and in the next four

Nearly 73,000 of these Grand Prix models were built in 1963. The scarce ones are nonautomatic—only one in twelve was ordered with syncromesh shift.

Front view shows typical divided grille favored by Pontiac above a very severe bumper totally without guards.

years created an entirely new image for Pontiac. First came achievements on the NASCAR tracks, then an impressive, if losing effort in the first Daytona 500 Grand National Race. By 1959 the engineers had developed their "toys" to be competitive with the best of the Chrysler muscle cars.

The stylists that would complete the turn-around came up with a lower, longer car in 1959 and made it five inches wider. Here is where commonality showed an Achilles heel: Buick and Olds had essentially the same body shells

and elected to continue with their current wheel tread. Knudsen had his Pontiac team bring the wheels all the way out. Thus was born "wide-track." The newly styled Pontiacs looked just right on the chassis, and handling was remarkably improved. Their sister GM cars looked a little like junior wearing Dad's pants, with the chassis appearing too narrow for the body they carried.

In 1962, Pontiac created a smaller luxury car by dropping the Bonneville engine, bucket seats, and sporty console into the Catalina and naming it the Grand Prix. Not surprisingly, over thirty thousand were sold this first year of the GP.

For 1963, the car was totally restyled with the somewhat fussy side panels of the 1962 made pure and simple. Headlights now were stacked in vertical pairs at the extreme outer edge of the

Headlights were stacked vertically in pairs, with the parking lights recessed into the sporty, open grille.

Grand Prix's badge was this modest racing-flag-derived GP medallion on the rear fender.

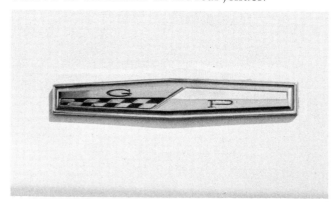

fenders, emphasizing the width of the Grand Prix. Inside was all the lush decor of the upper-line Bonneville, Morrokide upholstery, wood grain steering wheel and dash accents, and even a functional vacuum gauge on the glittering console. Sales soared to 72,000 and that in a year when the Buick showrooms featured the dazzling new Riviera. Many shoppers must have looked at both these luxury, sporty cars and decided the Grand Prix, at a thousand dollars less, was the better buy.

Tom McGuinness is the proud owner of our featured car. He found it in 1981 through a hobby publication ad. It was a one-owner original. with

The Grand Prix was as lushly upholstered as any Thunderbird. Morrokide was a leather look-alike and wore well. The instrument on the center console is a vacuum gauge.

just 42,000 miles logged and in dead storage some twelve years. Factory base price of the '63 GP was $3,490, but this car delivered at $4,622 according to the original bill of sale. The car has sport wheels and air conditioning. Tom flew to New Jersey, made the car as road ready as possible in the owner's garage, and drove it home safely to Ohio.

New shocks and springs were required, but the exhaust system was still sound. The 303 horsepower V-8 required a tune up with a rebuild of the carburetor—the only other work required under the hood. The original paint still shines, and all chrome is excellent.

Tom and his wife enjoy the Grand Prix and have acquired another of the same model to restore as well as a '65 Bonneville.

Other Pontiacs well worth looking at are the very popular GTO series introduced in 1964. While these are high-dollar cars, there are real sleepers in the big series Bonnevilles, such as the '59 and '63 through '65 convertibles.

1963 CHRYSLER CROWN IMPERIAL CONVERTIBLE COUPE

Chrysler Corporation used the Imperial designation on their top-of-the-line models from the very earliest days. The most exotic LeBaron custom-bodied phaetons offered in 1933 wore the Custom Imperial nameplate. The radical Airflow of 1934 was offered in a low-volume limo series bearing the Imperial name in addition to the high-volume four-door Chrysler model.

This practice continued through 1954 with the Imperial essentially a luxury trimmed Chrysler wearing a different grille. A dramatic change occurred in 1955 when the Imperial became an autonomous division of the Chrysler Corpora-

The 1963 Imperial featured a restrained front end and a subdued tail fin, reflecting a change from the more flamboyant earlier models.

tion. While it still shared components with the New Yorker line, it was quite a different car. The 1955–56 years saw a two-door and four-door hardtop introduced, in addition to the sedan and stretched wheelbase limos, last of these giants to be made in-house. From 1957 on, Ghia of Italy would handcraft each one from a kit that Chrysler would package and ship overseas.

Beginning in 1957 and ending in 1963, Imperial made a supreme effort to crack Cadillac's hold on the Park Avenue market. Surprisingly, they made their pitch on flamboyant style, as well as advanced engineering and a superb ride. One has to look at the 1958–60 Lincoln and the 1957–62 Cadillac before evaluating the extreme approach Imperial took. In those years, being extreme was popular. The big new 1957 models took awards both in America and in Europe for design excellence.

This profile view with top erected reveals the huge
size of the panoramic wraparound windshield.

With the top down and stowed under the boot, the
Imperial looks even longer than its actual 227
inches.

The soaring fins with exotic taillights, the shallow trunk sporting a fake continental wheel insert, the sunken headlamps, these would become the trademark of the Imperial until the Lincoln derived slab-sided models of the 1964 and 1965.

A small cult of admirers liked these expensive cars, and the high water mark in sales happened that first year of the new look, 1957. With over 37,000 sold they came within a whisker of matching Lincoln, but in later years they would settle into the 11,000 to 18,000 unit range. Our car shown, a 1963 model, sold a total of 14,108, all body styles included. Cadillac sold 163,174 cars in 1963.

If the flamboyant lines of this series of Imperials has appeal, it is surely strongest in the Crown convertibles. And here, surprisingly, were the very slowest sellers, with production ranging from 400 to 1,000 yearly. This 1963, for example, drew just 531 orders.

All Imperials were noted for remarkable handling, most critics giving them the edge over Cadillac and Lincoln because of the unique torsion-bar suspension the Imperial used. The three-speed Torqueflite automatic transmission was reputed to be the most rugged in the industry and, teamed with the big V-8, gave surprisingly good gas mileage.

Because of Chrysler's engineering reputation, the fine mechanics were taken for granted. The car was sold on its dramatic looks and on a mind-boggling list of standard equipment and exotic options to delight even the most jaded taste.

Imagine the driver's seat turning out on a swivel to greet you when you open the car door! Imagine a rear-view mirror that cuts the glare of a following car's headlights automatically by reacting to the heat of their beam! Plus, six-way power seats, auto pilot cruise control, foot-operated radio, multi-cycle windshield wipers, and the knowledge that when your choice of 178 color combinations was applied, the entire car body was wet sanded for hours by hand!

Rear deck ornament is a highly stylized bird in flight.

Imperials have birds everywhere. This 1963 hood ornament is still carried in reduced form on the 1984 Le Baron convertible.

This unusual headlight design was a nostalgic return to the separate lamps of the classic car age.

The proof of quality sometimes shows up best after gross neglect. I was shown a 1959 LeBaron Imperial a few years back that had just been hauled out of a decade of musty and damp storage. The fenders and rockers were rusted, of course, but everything inside still gleamed. No pits on the chrome, no rot in the fine fabrics, no cracks or warpage in the dash or steering wheel. A new battery was placed under the hood, and the dash switch turned on. Every one of the many interior lights glowed brightly, the radio played

from its multiple speakers. The engine needed just ten minutes to be purring. I still wonder why I passed up this potential gem, particularly at the 1976 asking price of $95.

The owner of the Crown convertible featured showed better judgment when she came across her car sitting in the sun at Sarasota, Florida. After searching for a sound and restorable Imperial convertible for three years, Marilyn Daniels took a long look at the perfect body shell of this 1963 and knew she was not likely to find a bet-

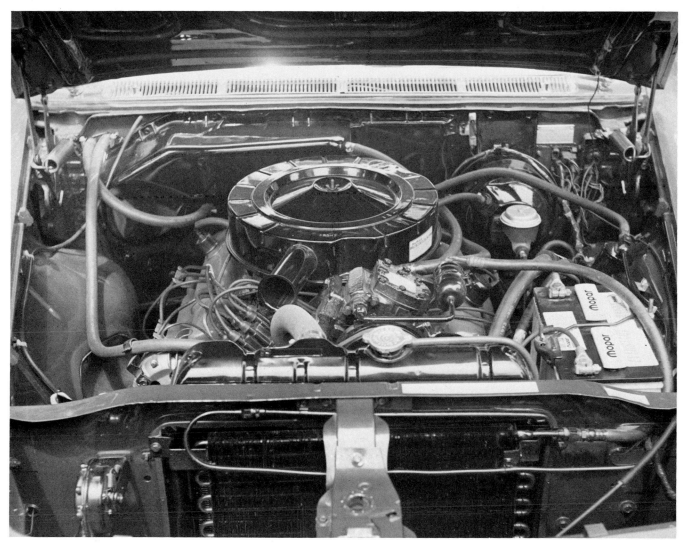

The Imperial's big V-8 produced 340 horsepower in the 1963 edition.

ter restoration candidate. Though the top was down and the interior looked like "worn shoes" as she puts it, though the paint was faded, and the mechanics unknown, she bought the car on the spot. The original bill of sale indicated the first owner paid exactly $5,782 for his big convertible—with no options. Even the Caddy convertible of 1963 was nearly $300 less, which partially explains Imperials's paltry sales.

The car was taken to a repair garage where it got new tires, a new dual exhaust system, and a new top. Some other minor work was done as well.

Impatient to return home to Ohio, Ms. Daniels started on her way still lacking a working horn, directionals, and power windows. Florida provided her thunderbumpers immediately, and Marilyn was grateful that the wipers were still operating as she drove through hours of torrential rain. Only three breakdowns later, Ms. Daniels had her Imperial at its new Ohio home. Her journey's adventures included a dead bat-

tery, fuel line problems that new filters cured, and faulty, dried out plug wires, heated and burnt, which she replaced.

Over the next year, the proud owner has had the front end overhauled—bushings were desperately needed. The 78,000 mile engine required only a major tune up. Then followed an interminable series of items: new directional switches, a horn switch, three power window motors, a new radio speaker, a windshield washer pump, rebuilding the carb and the factory air, and replacing the freeze plugs. Then back to the engine to replace some valve guide seals. Finally, a recurring bucking problem, eventually solved by a new fuel pump. A new dash clock to help her keep track of all these fun hours about wrapped up the mechanics. A totally new brake job and refinishing the car in Claret metallic red made the machine ready for its visit to the upholstery shop. With a new interior in correct Alabaster white leather, the restored car took a second-place award its first time out and shortly after, an Ohio best-in-show plaque.

Marilyn Daniels drives her Imperial often, logging over three thousand miles annually, and reports the 4,720-pound car delivers 17 MPG on the highway and 12 MPG around town. She chose Goodyear American Eagles because she wanted the wear and safety of a premium radial and because it has the correct whitewall width of the 1963 tire originally offered.

As I've stated elsewhere, Imperial sedans and hardtops are, in my opinion, the great sleeper values in the old-car hobby, particularly those made between 1957 and 1968. Decent cars can

Imperial wheel covers are distinctive and hard to find in such flawless condition. Whitewall width is correct for 1963.

be found in that rock bottom range of from $500 to $1,000. Some of my particular favorites would be in the $1,000-to-$3,000 range, and they would include the '53, '54, '55, and '56 two-door Newport and Southampton hardtops, the earlier '51 and '52 fluid drive hardtops, and of course the great open-highway yachts, the converts of 1957 through 1968.

Now where did I put that note about the man in Colorado who is selling a 1960 Crown Imperial convertible out of twelve years storage, says it will run. . . .

Huge front fenders and grille-support sheet metal were prone to rust inside. Any Snowbelt car should be carefully inspected prior to purchase. This Florida car posed no such restoration problem.

Probably the most tasteful rear end styling of an Imperial since 1956. Backup lights are carried in the bumper.

1963 FORD THUNDERBIRD HARDTOP COUPE

The saga of the T'bird is quite remarkable in that every model made, from the first 1955 two seater, to the last coupe of 1966, is being avidly collected by thousands of Ford fanatics. The four-door versions of 1967–1971 are even now slowly gaining adherents, despite T'bird's having became a totally different car about every three years.

The near-classic status of the original drop-top two seater, made from 1955 through 1957, is accepted far and wide. Many still wonder why Ford dropped the two-passenger for the bigger four-passenger "squareback" in 1958. The squared off, formal lines of that series ended in 1960. The 1961 model bore a striking similarity

The 1963 T'bird was again long and low, with a large greenhouse. The chrome hash marks on the door were new this year.

in approach to the new Continental, and that was not entirely accidental. Originally, the Lincoln had been intended by its designer, Elwood Engle, as a new Thunderbird. The proportions better suited a larger car, it was decided, and the design study changed names. The same man who led the styling of the '55 model, Bill Boyer, ended up having the largest input into the '61–'63 series.

The 1963 model illustrated is nearly identical to its 1961 cousin. Minor trim changes, including a set of chrome hash marks on the doors, are the most obvious update. Ford was fond of offering special editions, implying the exclusivity of a low-production car. In 1963 a special edition of the Thunderbird was introduced in Monaco, Morocco, sporting one color combination only: maroon with a white top and a snow white leather interior. Contrary to popular belief, they were made in fairly large numbers. The true

Knife-edge styling of fenders and headlamps
sunken in the grille are reminiscent of the 1961
Lincoln, though the lines here are less formal.

Ford and Thunderbird often featured oversize
taillights. These huge circular units were part of
the bumper and subject to parking-lot damage.

The Thunderbird interior resembles twin cockpits with considerable dash overhang. Full-length console was an integral design feature.

rarity among '63 Thunderbirds is the Sports Roadster variant. Only 455 of these factory customs were made. The roadster was Lee Iacocca's answer to dealers' requests for a new two seater. His bizarre solution was to drop in a huge molded fiberglass tonneau cover that effectively covered the whole rear passenger well of the four-seater convertible. Add those blinding Kelsey-Hayes chrome wire wheels, a front cockpit grab bar, a few special emblems, and *viola!* a new two seater. The tonneau cover had twin-hump fairings, one behind each front passenger and those lucky people could pretend they were up in a Sopwith Camel over the Western Front as they cruised down the highway.

The sports roadster at long last has become very, very popular, and forgeries abound.

You may not mind if yours is a recent conversion, but you surely don't want to pay the price of an original factory model. It is possible to obtain from Ford (or the various Thunderbird clubs) the serial numbers of those rare authen-

Lincoln and Thunderbird styling were closely related from 1961 on. Compare this view of the 1963 T'bird with the front of the 1961 Continental.

Thunderbird dash was always well-instrumented, part of the sports car image the car was intended to convey.

Trunk is extremely wide but shallow. The spare is not very accessible and awkward to remove.

tic models. All the components are available today to convert the standard convertible into a roadster, although at considerable cost. Back in those golden days, I once spoke to a Volkswagen dealer who offered me, in scornful terms, a Ford "gas hog" recently traded on the popular beetle. The year was 1969, the Ford a 1962 T'bird factory sports roadster. Its condition was immaculate, and the price $750. It sat unsold for many months, as I recall.

The model illustrated is the hardtop version most often found. It is a car of superior handling and fine workmanship. It was built in Ford's Wixom, Michigan, plant, where quality control in the early sixties was probably the highest to be found both in America and abroad. It had had one owner since 1963 and had been driven in the "salt belt" every winter. That careful owner had the underbody cleaned and oil sprayed every

The big 390 V-8 has been totally detailed by the owner, even down to new, correct decals.

fall. It is totally free of rust, and the chrome and paint gleam as though new.

Owner Craig Badger has had to do very little to bring his Thunderbird to show condition. Some years ago it was given a quality repaint in the original dark blue. The factory leather interior is mint, as is all its chrome. Craig, however, removed all engine accessories and totally detailed the engine compartment. When he obtained the car in 1980, it showed 76,000 miles, and in three years at its new home it has been driven just 4,000 additional miles.

On the day in 1980 when Mr. Badger acquired the car, the lady owner followed him to her garage and asked if she could get behind the wheel one last time. She backed it down the drive and handed the keys to its new owner. Cherish a fine car for seventeen years, and certainly the tears will flow—as hers did that day.

Landau bars serve as decoration on several postwar cars. Stylists like their nostalgic link with the classic car age, when they served a real function in raising and lowering a fabric top.

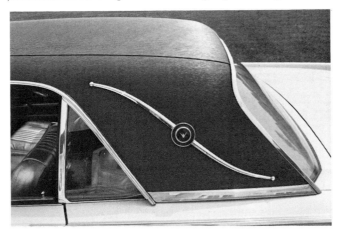

170

1964 PLYMOUTH SPORTS FURY CONVERTIBLE COUPE
(Factory super stock)

Looking up production figures can usually help in determining how many are left of a given model. Although auto insurers will tell you that perhaps 1 percent remain of cars older than twenty years, this becomes meaningless when applied to the performance cars of the fifties and sixties. So many varied combinations of engines, transmissions, and running gear were available, one model might have been set up twenty different ways, producing twenty different cars.

The Belvedere body in convertible form has a rakish look, befitting its startling performance in the Super Stock version.

This Sports Fury is surely the rarest among the rare. How many of the 3,858 listed 1964 convertibles have an engine built by the famed Unser brothers? How many have the entire front clip, fenders, hood, bumper, and splash pan in factory *aluminum?* How many attain 60 MPH from zero in under six seconds?

The factory offered the Sports Fury convertible with the 426 engine turning out 365 horses via a four-speed manual gearbox with Hurst linkage. Suspension was heavy duty with torsion bars up front and an anti-roll bar in the rear. Brakes were big 11-inch drums all around, body and frame were of unitized construction.

The Plymouth Fury started as an offshoot of the 1957 Belvedere line. The biggest V-8 then

Rear end is heavily chromed for a Plymouth. Grille design is repeatred between the taillight housings.

Trim on the Fury is bold and brightly enameled in red, white, and blue.

Head-on view is almost prosaic, giving little indication of the power beneath the plain hood.

Only the deck lid "Sports Fury" script tells you it's different from its plain-Jane six-cylinder cousin.

There is plenty of room in this Sports Fury. The seats are designed for boulevard cruising rather than the shaped buckets suited for high-speed driving.

Enameled side trim is picked up again on the deck lid, repeating the color theme.

offered produced 290 horsepower from a cast-iron block of 317-cubic-inch displacement. By 1959, Chrysler had sold twenty-five thousand hardtops and convertibles with the Sports Fury plate, delighting those who demanded performance with a capital *P*.

Motor Trend reviewed the road manners of a '64 Fury hardtop in January of that year and calmly agreed it would attain 130 MPH and turn the quarter-mile at 95 MPH!

Tom Schweitzer found his Fury convertible in California. It had been a high mileage car totally restored at considerable cost from the pan up. Tom delights in its look but says driving it takes some getting used to. He admits to many

The 426 power plant has been totally rebuilt to factory specs, and every accessory is stock on this model.

temptations when a Porsche or 'Vette pulls up next to him at a traffic light. Knowing he could be in the next county while they are shifting out of second brings a certain smile to his face. So far he has not yielded to that temptation.

If the performance potential of this Sports Fury appeals to you, you may be on your way to "Mopar mania." Chrysler wrote the book on muscle cars, starting with the legendary letter cars in 1955, then branched out with the "Cudas and Chargers." True performance cars are almost a hobby unto themselves. Here is where joining the appropriate club can greatly accelerate your knowledge of a highly specialized area of the old-car hobby.

The 426 badge is proudly stated in a geometric hood ornament on the Sports Fury.

176

1966 FORD MUSTANG CONVERTIBLE V-8

One can almost safely say the Mustang of 1965–66 is the most collectible postwar car around. Just don't say it at a Chevy car meet. The pony car of Lee Iacocca not only broke all first-year sales records when it sold 418,000 units in just twelve months, but it also staggered the clay-model planners at GM. Firebirds and Camaros would eventually enter the running and do well, but for a few years Ford's mighty Mustang was unchallenged.

Why was this car such a stunning success when other personal, sporty-type cars had come before and gone nowhere? The market was ready for a low-priced machine that could go briskly, could be optioned with everything except an electric waffle iron, and could be ordered as both a hardtop *and* a convertible. The Mustang success pointed up how badly Studebaker had miscalculated ten years before when the Loewy coupes were not offered as convertibles.

The wide range of engines, transmissions, interiors, and varied appearance options let the buyer, in effect, design his own car. Even today, at Mustang meets it is virtually impossible to find two nearly identical cars. Options, besides delighting customers, are the way to profits, we've been told.

Comfortable for four adults, the car is only 181.6 inches long, nearly two feet shorter than most six-passenger sedans of 1965, the wheelbase a modest 108 inches. (Studebaker's sporty Hawks sat on a chassis of 120-inch W.B.) Only 51 inches high, passengers sat low in the car,

The classic formula at work: long hood and short rear deck. The body crease culminating in a fake air scoop adds to the apparent length of the compact Mustang.

The sporty Mustang look that took the country by storm. Without the galloping pony on the grille, it might have come from an Italian styling studio.

Like many auto designs that remain in production for several years, the first is usually the best. Collectors agree that the '65 and '66 models are most popular.

Top stowed away, the Mustang's clean lines are evident.

Part of the American flavor, the galloping Mustang on the grille is repeated on the optional seat covers, where it is embossed in the vinyl.

"Knock-off" hub wheel covers were a rare find in new condition. Accessories such as these add considerably in dressing up a car correctly.

Simulated air scoop looks as though it were intended to cool feverish brake drums.

making for good stability. Unfortunately, this also made for increased road noise. Body insulation was not one of the Mustang's strong points. The early six-cylinder model rode on 13-inch tires, and Ford wisely upgraded all models to the larger 6.95-by-14 size in 1966.

It may seem irrelevant to consider the car's styling when total marketplace acceptance speaks volumes. I personally wish it were not so busy, particularly along the sides. It is sobering to reflect that more 1966 convertible Mustangs, *alone*, were sold than all the Hawks and sport coupes offered by Studebaker in a decade.

The V-8 convert listed at $2,759, and that could easily exceed $3,000 if one added the sporty and useful luggage rack, the Decor Group, which put wild ponies embossed on your seat backs and a nearly real wooden wheel in your hands. Three-speed Cruise-A-Matic was an option, and V-8 power choices ranged from 200 to 271 horses. The shift lever could be floor mounted or in a full-length center console.

Ford's popular 289 is dressed for show, but beneath the glitter are rings and valves that have seen 100,000 miles come and go.

Virtually every needed part of a Mustang interior is available to today's restorer. This restored example does not show its years or miles.

One of the obvious reasons for the popularity of the Mustang as a restorer's choice is the plentiful supply. Over one million were made of the first, and most desirable, style from mid-1964 to late 1966. With such demand and interest, it was natural for reproduction firms to spring up and strive to meet the demand for parts. The Mustang was certainly no less prone, and perhaps more than some, to rust in its more hidden recesses. Today, virtually every stamping and panel of this car is being reproduced. It is probably the one case where having a parts car may not pay, since many parts of *both* cars are probably bad.

Again, in the discussion of good body, bad mechanics versus badly rotted body with good mechanics, the Mustang choice is clear. I believe it is wiser to go with the solid body and to restore the mechanics as needed.

Our fine example was purchased by Dennis Bowsher as a nearly new used car back in 1968. The clock showed 18,000 miles, and Dennis gladly paid $1,800 for his Mustang. Then he proceeded to drive it—to Texas, to Mississippi, to Ohio. One day he realized his beautiful car was getting weary. With 94,000 miles now showing, it was getting difficult to close the doors. Open a door, and the car would gratefully sag in on its now somewhat rubbery frame. With massive salt spray corrosion underneath, all the torque boxes were beginning to resemble Irish lace. Still, the drive train was bearing up fine. Dennis decided a restoration would give him a new car, and although he admits sentiment played a part, the practical dollar investment seemed valid.

This was several years ago, before all those repro parts hit the market. Hamilton Auto Restoration had to do it the hard way: patching, replacing frame rails, and fabricating torque boxes from scratch. It took almost five months, but the finished car justified the effort. Now showing over 112,000 miles on the odometer, this Mustang gets regular exercise.

Restored before repro body-panel parts were available, much shop work was necessary to hand fabricate new torque boxes and floor pan inserts on this high-mileage Mustang.

With so much replaced, Dennis likes to point out that the fuel pump and water pump are original, and that the rugged 289 is still going strong on the factory rings and valves.

Obviously, the model of choice among Mustangs is the first convertible. The one seldom seen is the 260-cubic-inch V-8. In fact, many of the early sixes were switched by later owners to the 289 V-8. Finding a rust-free model is half the battle, because there is not the usual elusive search for parts. No other old car has such a cottage industry supporting it as Iacocca's wonder car.

1967 PLYMOUTH BELVEDERE GTX HARDTOP

From at least the mid-thirties there has been in every car company (except possibly the Checker Cab Company) an engineer who speculates: "What would happen if I put our biggest engine in our smallest car?"

Back in the thirties, Buick did just that, putting their bigger engine in a lighter chassis and calling it the Century. Over the years the peppy Century became known as the "banker's hotrod." In the postwar period when gas was as plentiful and as cheap as water, many buyers called for performance. Auto racing was becoming the number one spectator sport in America, and thousands wanted, however impractical, to have street autos capable of blinding acceleration and high speed. Whether the public was following the stock-car racing scene, or that kind of racing was following the public, is hard to say.

Detroit's answer was that if the public wanted more power, they would produce it. Chrysler led with the '300' letter dynasty, from 1955 to 1966. John DeLorean, heading the Pontiac Division at GM, followed with the potent GTOs. Every company believed the way to sell their stock sedan to Dad was to produce a highway cannonball Junior would drool over, if only from afar.

The competition was fierce and resulted in a huge number of cars we now blanket with the generic term "muscle car."

Among the least known of the sixties' muscle cars, the GTX was a great value in its day and is a "sleeper" collectible now.

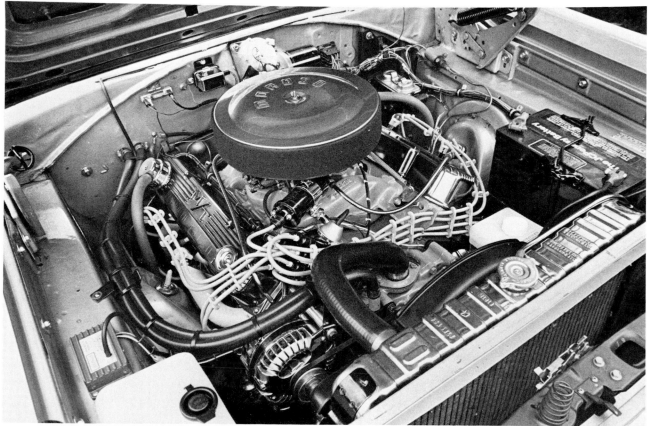

Racing stripes and twin hood scoops make the 1967 GTX instantly identifiable.

Full instrumentation, including a tachometer, was part of the GTX package. Note the shaped-to-fit shift lever on the floor.

Slavishly detailed to perfection, the GTX engine room looks as it did when it left the factory.

The Chrysler Corporation had their Chargers, Satellites, Demons, Roadrunners, Barracudas, and Furys. One of the lesser-known Chrysler products is our example of a muscle car, the GTX.

Built on the frame of a prosaic intermediate Belvedere, the GTX was a high-performance luxury hardtop. In their ads, Chrysler stated: "Cubic inches aren't everything." This was usually run above a huge rendering of the GTX hood ornament, which sported a prominent "440" in its center. Chrysler wanted you to know they had plenty of those inches. The Belvedere, which in its basic form as a family car ran well on a modest six cylinder, was offered with two engine choices as a GTX. A big wedgehead V-8

of 440 cubes and 480 feet of torque, or, for those who hated to see the "300s" go, a street hemi at 426 cubes and 490 feet of torque. That second choice put out a mere 425 horsepower. If you wanted to put cleats on the car and run it up the side of the Empire State Building, it was just the thing.

The ads also said the GTX was "a well-rounded supercar." That was undeniably true, as a heavy-duty suspension was standard, with heavier ball-joints, stiffer torsion bars, and firmer shocks and springs. Shifters offered were a special high-upshift Torqueflite automatic or a four-speed for the purist.

Add bucket seat, hood scoops, optional disc brakes, special red streak tires, sport stripes, and, to cap it off, a Pit Stop quick-fill gas cap. Most of this equipment was functional and made a car with so much power highly roadable. In addition, the interior was as lush as an Olds "98."

What was remarkable was that this opulent powerhouse cost just $3,178 with most of the advertised features standard. Considering that was just $1,000 more than a stripped Valiant, it is surprising more weren't sold. Just about 2,300 went out the door, and a miniscule 300 of those were the now wildly sought after convertible GTX.

Wheelbase is 116 inches; overall length, 200 inches, as with all cars from the Belvedere family. But the road-ready GTX weighs over 3,600 pounds, thanks to all that road-holding, high-speed plumbing.

If you have a serious interest in finding and restoring a muscle car of the sixties, or just want a sporty two-door personal car (Firebird, Camaro,

Hardtop roofline of the GTX is oddly asymetrical, giving it a frail look.

later Mustang, etc.), I strongly suggest you study the production charts first. You may acquire a truly rare and desirable car that will appreciate far more over a five- or ten-year period than you might think.

The Plymouth Road Runner of 1968–70 saw fewer than 3,000 convertibles made, just 824 in 1970. The 1969 Barracuda convertible was made in only 1,442 editions. The early Sports Fury converts of 1959 saw almost 6,000 sold but are almost unknown today. Find one and treasure it!

Stuart Middleton is the young man who found and treasures the GTX featured. He is the third owner of this show car, which was in superb original condition when Stuart located and purchased it in 1978. To make it flawless, Stuart removed all engine accessories and detailed the engine compartment. Every accessory was either replated or repainted to factory specs. The auto has never been operated in winter since new. The original owner was so taken with the GTX, he owned two identical cars, one to preserve and one to drive. The preserved car is the one Mr. Middleton was lucky enough to acquire.

Rear fender treatment is striking. The GTX shares the concave body wall treatment with the senior Chrysler line.

The interior decor, in style and quality, is worthy of Lincoln. GTX emblem is placed discreetly between the seat backs.

Clubs in the Old-Car Hobby

From the earliest days of the hobby, people of like interest banded together to foster the restoration of antique autos. The original handful of clubs in the thirties has grown to well over a thousand today. The following is a selection of both multiple-marque clubs and one-marque clubs. This list is tilted toward clubs with a strong interest in postwar American cars and is by no means complete. See such directories as *Hemmings Vintage Auto Almanac* for the most thorough compilation available. Remember, too, that many of the larger clubs have scores of regional chapters.

Antique Automobile Club of America
501 West Governor Road
PO Box 417
Hershey, PA 17033

Classic Car Club of America
PO Box 443
Madison, NJ 07940

Contemporary Historical Vehicle Association
PO Box 40
Antioch, TN 37031

Horseless Carriage Club of America
9031 E. Florence Ave.
Downey, CA 90240

Milestone Car Society
PO Box 50850
Indianapolis, IN 46250

Veteran Motor Car Club of America
105 Elm St.
Andover, MA 01810

While many of these larger, multi-marque clubs were originally formed around earlier periods of automotive development, all wlcome the post-war car in specific categories at their meets and on tours. Typically, dues will range from $10 to $36 annually and include monthly newsletters, colorful quarterly magazines, or both.

Some One-Marque Clubs

American Motors Owners Association
PO Box 232
Kewaunee, WI 54216

Buick Club of America
PO Box 898
Garden Grove, CA 92642

Cadillac Club International
PO Box 1
Palm Springs, CA 92263

Cadillac LaSalle Club, Inc.
3340 Poplar Drive
Warren, MI 48091

Classic Chevy Club, International
PO Box 17188
Orlando, FL 32810

Classic Thunderbird Club, International
10315 Jefferson Blvd.
PO Box 2398
Culver City, CA 90230

Corvair Society of America
PO Box 2488
Pensacola, FL 32503

Hudson Essex Terraplane Club, Inc.
100 E. Cross St.
Ypsilanti, MI 48197

Imperial Owners Club
PO Box 991
Scranton, PA 18503

Lincoln Continental Owners Club
PO Box 549
Nogales, AZ 85621

Mustang Club of America, Inc.
PO Box 447
Lithonia, GA 30058

The Nash Club of America
R No. 1 Box 253
Clinton, IA 52732

National Corvette Owners Association
PO Box 777A
Falls Church, VA 22046

National Nomad Club
4691 S. Mariposa Drive
Englewood, CO 80110

The Oldsmobile Club of America, Inc.
145 Latona Road
Rochester, NY 14626

The Packard Club
PO Box 2808
Oakland, CA 94618

Packards International Motor Car Club
302 French St.
Santa Ana, CA 92701

Shelby American Automobile Club
22 Olmstead
West Redding, CT 06896

Studebakers Drivers Club
PO Box 3044
South Bend, IN 46619

The Willys Club
1850 Valley Forge Road
Lansdale, PA 19446

WPC Club (Chrysler products)
PO Box 4705
N. Hollywood, CA 91607

Some Valuable Reference Works

The old-car hobbyist will seek out his particular car's shop manual and owner's manual, whether original or a reprint. Sales literature is valuable reference material, and the collecting of these original showroom pamphlets and brochures is a hobby in itself.

Original reference works on old cars are often hard to find and frequently expensive. Here is a short list of modern reference works the author believes will prove invaluable to both neophyte and experienced hobbyists:

Encyclopedia of American Cars 1940–1970 and *Complete Book of Collectable Cars 1940–1980:* Both of the above books are by Richard M. Langworth and the editors of *Consumers Guide.* Both are detailed and exhaustive, with considerable auto company history and recommendations of specific cars.

Encyclopedia of American Cars 1946 to 1959, Moloney and Dammann, Crestline Publishing: Thousands of factory photos are compiled in this volume of the Crestline series, along with details on features and original prices and specifications.

Hemmings' Vintage Auto Almanac: This soft-cover publication of *Hemmings Motor News* is a directory to suppliers, clubs, museums, and wrecking yards. Well-organized for ready reference.

Standard Catalog of American Cars 1946–1975: A massive 700-plus–page encyclopedia of vital statistics pertaining to all American cars of the period. Production figures, price guide by condition, serial numbers, and 1,500 photos—all aid in providing quick answers to questions that constantly arise in the hobby. A publication of Old Cars Weekly available through Krause Publications, Iola, Wisconsin.

These are just a few of the thousands of titles available today on collected cars. Half a dozen national book distributors specialize in the old-car field and run extensive advertising in the periodicals listed next.

Some Useful Publications for the Do-It-Yourself Restorer

These publications may be ordered, by title and author, through the larger book distributors that advertise in the old-car hobby press.

Auto Restoration: From Junker to Jewel, by Mills ($15.95).

Auto Restoration Tips & Techniques, by Murray ($5.95). A well-illustrated, soft-cover introduction to old-car restoration from Petersen Books.

Automobile Sheet Metal Repair, by Robert Sargent ($12.50).

Car Interior Restoration, by Terry Boyce ($3.95).

Chiltons Auto Repair Manual 1940–53 ($19.95).

Chiltons Auto Repair Manual 1954–63 ($19.95). The Chilton reprints of the garage mechanic's bible cover most postwar American cars and are invaluable.

Corvette Restoration: State of the Art, by Antonick ($29.95).

Corvair: A History & Restoration Guide, by Artzbeger ($19.95).

Essentials of Upholstery & Trim for Vintage & Classic Cars, by Locke ($15.00).

How to Restore Your Mustang (1965–1968 Models), by Dobbs ($14.95).

The Mustang Encyclopedia—Consumers Guide ($12.95).

Restoration & Preservation of Vintage and Classic Cars, by Wood ($19.95).

The Restoration of Antique and Classic Cars, by Wheatley and Morgan ($10.95). A British classic, useful as a general introduction to the many skills necessary to the restorer.

Skinned Knuckles ($10.00 per year). While other hobby periodicals will occasionally run a restoration technique article, this monthly magazine is devoted solely to the subject. A subscription or sample copy may be ordered from: Skinned Knuckles, 175 May Ave., Monrovia, California 91016.

Some Leading Periodicals on Old Cars

Automobile Quarterly
245 W. Main St.
Kutztown, PA 19530

The Cadillac of old-car magazines, published in hard cover, horizontal format. Writing and color photography without peer. By subscription only and moderately expensive.

Car Collector and Car Classics
PO Box 28571
Atlanta, GA 30328

A monthly, much color photography, feature articles on American and foreign collectible cars.

Car & Parts Magazine
PO Box 482
Sidney, OH 45367

Average 200-page monthly with articles, stories, and technical tips. About two-thirds devoted to classified ads, hence its title.

Hemmings Motor News
PO Box 100
Bennington, VT 05201

This is the "bible" of the hobby. On the day Hemmings arrives in the mail, tens of thousands of Americans go into seclusion for three or four hours. It is simply the largest classified ad compilation sent out between two covers monthly. Large format, its 500-plus pages cover not only every aspect of the hobby including cars and parts for sale, divided by make, but every esoteric service from wheelwright to those who reproduce woodgrain dashboards. Most hobbyists feel Hemmings is indispensable.

Old Cars Weekly
700 E. State Street
Iola, WI 54945

Old Cars Weekly is the newspaper of the hobby. While it has a large classified section in its 64 tabloid-size pages, it is also unrivaled in its coverage of old-car auctions, museum events, famous-car sales, and other news of interest to the old-car buff.

Old Car Price Guide

Published by Krause, the Wisconsin firm that puts out *Old Cars Weekly, Price Guide* is the most ambitious attempt to keep abreast of the changing market place of collectible cars. It has a quarterly soft-cover magazine format, available on newsstands and by subscription.

Special Interest Autos
Box 196
Bennington, VT 05201

A bi-monthly, features outstanding articles on collected cars from the classic era through the sixties. Particularly useful are their "driver-reports," in which a particular car is thoroughly analyzed. Classified ads are a minor part of this magazine.